Wellington's Infantry

Wellington's Infantry

British Foot Regiments 1800–1815

Gabriele Esposito

Pen & Sword
MILITARY

First published in Great Britain in 2021 by
Pen & Sword Military
An imprint of
Pen & Sword Books Ltd
Yorkshire – Philadelphia

Copyright © Gabriele Esposito 2021

ISBN 978 1 52678 667 8

The right of Gabriele Esposito to be identified as
Author of this Work has been asserted by him in accordance
with the Copyright, Designs and Patents Act 1988.

A CIP catalogue record for this book is
available from the British Library

All rights reserved. No part of this book may be reproduced or
transmitted in any form or by any means, electronic or mechanical
including photocopying, recording or by any information storage and
retrieval system, without permission from the Publisher in writing.

Typeset in Ehrhardt
by Mac Style

Printed and bound in India by Replika Press Pvt. Ltd.

Pen & Sword Books Limited incorporates the imprints of Atlas, Archaeology, Aviation, Discovery, Family History, Fiction, History, Maritime, Military, Military Classics, Politics, Select, Transport, True Crime, Air World, Frontline Publishing, Leo Cooper, Remember When, Seaforth Publishing, The Praetorian Press, Wharncliffe Local History, Wharncliffe Transport, Wharncliffe True Crime and White Owl.

For a complete list of Pen & Sword titles please contact

PEN & SWORD BOOKS LIMITED
47 Church Street, Barnsley, South Yorkshire, S70 2AS, England
E-mail: enquiries@pen-and-sword.co.uk
Website: www.pen-and-sword.co.uk

Or

PEN AND SWORD BOOKS
1950 Lawrence Rd, Havertown, PA 19083, USA
E-mail: Uspen-and-sword@casematepublishers.com
Website: www.penandswordbooks.com

Contents

Acknowledgements		vii
Introduction		viii
Chapter 1	The Foot Guards	1
Chapter 2	The Line Infantry	9
Chapter 3	The Scottish Infantry	24
Chapter 4	The Light Infantry	29
Chapter 5	Royal Veteran Battalions and Fencible Regiments	50
Chapter 6	The British Troops in Canada	58
Chapter 7	The British Troops in the West Indies	72
Chapter 8	The British Troops in Africa and Australia	82
Chapter 9	The British Troops in India	87
Chapter 10	Foreign Troops in British Service	94
Chapter 11	The King's German Legion	103
Chapter 12	Uniforms and Equipment	110
Bibliography		135
Index		136

Gabriele Esposito is a military historian who works as a freelance author and researcher for some of the most important publishing houses in the military history sector. In particular, he is an expert specializing in uniformology: his interests and expertise range from the ancient civilizations to modern post-colonial conflicts. During recent years he has conducted and published several researches on the military history of the Latin American countries, with special attention to the War of the Triple Alliance and the War of the Pacific. He is among the leading experts on the military history of the Italian Wars of Unification and the Spanish Carlist Wars. His books and essays are published on a regular basis by Osprey Publishing, Winged Hussar Publishing and Libreria Editrice Goriziana; he is also the author of numerous military history articles appearing in specialized magazines like *Ancient Warfare Magazine*, *Medieval Warfare Magazine*, *The Armourer*, *History of War*, *Guerres et Histoire*, *Focus Storia* and *Focus Storia Wars*.

Acknowledgements

This book is dedicated to my parents, Maria Rosaria and Benedetto, for all the great support that they give me during the creation of my books. Thanks to their precious advice of 'veteran' teachers, my researches are clearly much better. A very special thanks goes to Philip Sidnell, the commissioning editor of my books for Pen & Sword: this new series, which starts with the present book, exists thanks to his great intelligence and positive vision. Everything began with a simple idea, during a very hot summer: now that project is coming to fruition. Last but not least, a special mention goes to the production manager of this title, Matt Jones, for his great competence. All the pictures published in this book are public domain ones obtained from the magnificent Digital Collections of the Brown University Library, in particular from the incredible Anne S.K. Brown Military Collection. The vast contents of the latter can be easily browsed at: https://library.brown.edu/info/collections/askb/prints/

Introduction

The main aim of this book is to present a detailed overview of the organization, uniforms and equipment of the British infantry during the Napoleonic Period. The period taken into account in the present work coincides with one of the most glorious moments in the military history of Britain, during which the British Army fought around the globe to counter the expansionist ambitions of Napoleon and his newly established French Empire. After the Peace of Amiens was broken in 1803, Great Britain found itself at war with an old enemy (France), but also with a new competitor (Napoleon): the latter was the greatest military commander of his times, a man who was able to transform the French Army into the most lethal fighting machine of the early nineteenth century. The war experiences of 1793–1803 had not been very positive ones for the British Army, which was still recovering from the crushing defeats suffered during the American War of Independence and badly needed to be reformed in order to become more efficient and modern. At the turn of the new century, Britain was still the greatest colonial power in the world and could count on the most formidable navy in the world; on land, however, its army was too weak to confront the French on anything like equal terms. The British land forces did not have a great leader comparable to Napoleon and were still influenced by tactical models that had been outclassed by events. During the Napoleonic Wars, the British military apparatus did its best to improve, especially under the guidance of intelligent officers who belonged to a 'new generation'. These innovative and capable men reformed the British Army by improving its standards of service and creating a new relationship – based on mutual trust – with the men under their command. Wellington was the greatest of these officers, one of the few European generals who had the personal capabilities to take on Napoleon in an effective way: it was he who 'forged' the new British Army by fighting against the French in the Iberian Peninsula from 1808–14. After learning from experience, the British soldiers were finally able to face Napoleon over the Belgian fields of Waterloo and thus write the last page of a glorious military epic. Waterloo, however, was just the final result of a long process. During the period from 1800–15, in fact, British officers had to completely reform the tactical and operational patterns of their units: for example, a real 'light infantry revolution' took place among the ranks of the foot troops. All this was an experimental process, which sometimes led to bad results. The glorious actions of the Peninsula, indeed, were not the only ones fought between 1800 and 1815. We should not forget, for example, the three campaigns conducted in the Netherlands (1799, 1809 and 1814), which were disasters for the British Army.

To follow the evolution of the British Army during the Napoleonic Period, we have divided the text into twelve chapters. The first one will deal with the elite of the British infantry, the three regiments of Foot Guards, while the second will analyze the general organization of the line infantry, with its 104 Regiments of Foot serving during the Napoleonic Wars. The third chapter will be devoted to the Scottish troops (both Highlanders and Lowlanders), since they had many distinctive features, and the fourth will focus on the light infantry and will reconstruct the crucially important 'light infantry revolution' mentioned above. The fifth chapter will deal with two little-known categories of foot troops which had important roles in 'static' defence: the Royal Veteran Battalions and the Fencible Regiments. The sixth chapter will reconstruct the British military presence in Canada, an area where the War of 1812 against the United States took place, while the seventh will analyze the British military units deployed in the crucial region of the West Indies, where several actions were fought against the French. The eighth will discuss the British military presence in the early colonies of Africa and Australia, where Great Britain was still struggling to establish permanent settlements, and the ninth will describe the military forces of the East India Company, which were not part of the regular British Army but which fought for the commercial interests of the Crown in India. The tenth chapter will cover all the 'foreign' troops serving in the British Army during the Napoleonic Wars, the eleventh will deal with the most formidable of the latter, the King's German Legion, and the last chapter will describe the uniforms and equipment employed by all the categories of foot troops covered in the previous chapters.

Chapter 1

The Foot Guards

All the European armies of the early nineteenth century comprised a certain number of guard units, which made up an elite inside the military forces of each country. These could be small bodyguard corps, having as their main function that of escorting the monarchs, or larger combatant units with superior training and morale. In Britain, the Royal Guard had a very long tradition and consisted of units belonging to the second category, i.e. combatant corps having a 'special' status and performing peculiar duties. The infantry component of the British Royal Guard consisted of three regiments: the 1st Foot Guards or Grenadier Guards, the 2nd Foot Guards or Coldstream Guards and the 3rd Foot Guards or Scots Guards. Each of these three infantry units had a distinguished history, from which their nicknames came.

The 1st Foot Guards was created in 1665 by merging together two infantry regiments that already had guard status and duties: Lord Wentworth's Regiment and John Russell's Regiment. The first had been raised in 1656 by the future Charles II during his exile in the Spanish Netherlands (present-day Belgium), and initially consisted of professional soldiers who had followed the future monarch into exile and were loyal to the Stuarts. With the Restoration in 1660, the unit came back to England and became part of the reorganized English Army. John Russell's Regiment was created in 1660, after Charles II returned to England; it mirrored the functions and structure of Lord Wentworth's Regiment and thus soon became a duplicate of the latter unit. In 1665, it was decided to unite the two guard regiments into a single unit, which received the new denomination of 1st Regiment of Foot Guards. The unified unit adopted its famous nickname of Grenadier Guards only in 1815, following a Royal Proclamation that transformed the regiment into a grenadier corps. From the late seventeenth century, the military units defined as 'grenadier' ones enjoyed a superior status, since this denomination was peculiar of the heavy infantry corps which had special training and equipment. During the Napoleonic Wars, the famous French grenadiers of Napoleon's Imperial Guard became the most famous heavy infantrymen in the world due to their courage and discipline; when they were defeated at Waterloo by the British 1st Foot Guards, the latter unit was honoured with the new denomination of Grenadier Guards that it still retains today. As is clear from the above, until 1815, the 1st Foot Guards was a line infantry unit (albeit with 'guard' status) and not a grenadier one.

Officer of the 1st Foot Guards, 1815. This was the new uniform adopted by the unit soon after the Battle of Waterloo, when it became a grenadier corps. Note the golden lace on the collar, cuffs and frontal plastron (consisting of the lapels folded back, in order to show the regiment's distinctive colour).

The 2nd Foot Guards was created in 1650 as one of the infantry regiments that made up Cromwell's New Model Army. Initially known as Monck's Regiment of Foot, it supported the Restoration of the Stuarts in 1660 and made an epic march of five weeks from Coldstream (in Berwickshire) to London in order to sustain Charles II. Due to this episode, it soon received the nickname of Coldstream Guards from the village where the elite infantrymen had started their march. After the Restoration, the regiment remained in London to keep order in the capital; in 1661, due to its loyalty towards Charles II, it received the new official denomination of The Lord General's Regiment of Foot Guards. The 2nd Foot Guards was older than the 1st Foot Guards, but was placed as the second senior regiment of the Household Troops because it had entered royal service after the Grenadier Guards (until 1661, from a formal point of view, it had been part of the New Model Army and not of the royal forces). To underline the fact that their corps was older than the 1st Foot Guard, members of the Coldstream Guards adopted as their regimental motto the phrase '*Nulli Secundus*' ('Second to None'). In 1670, the unit adopted its definitive denomination of the Coldstream Regiment of Foot Guards.

The 3rd Foot Guards was actually the oldest of the three guard regiments, but was the last to enter English royal service; as a result, it was placed as the third senior unit of the Household Troops. The regiment was created in 1642, as part of the Scottish Army and not the English one. It should be remembered that until 1707, the Scottish military forces remained independent from their English equivalent since England and Scotland were two autonomous kingdoms. Charles I, as King of Scotland, ordered the formation of what was to become the 3rd Foot Guards in order to face the Irish Rebellion of 1641. The unit was raised by the Marquess of Argyll, Archibald Campbell, thus having as its first denomination that of the Marquis of Argyll's Royal Regiment. In 1650, when Charles II became King of Scotland following the execution of his father, the unit became a guard one and adopted the new title of Lyfe Guard of Foot. In 1651, following Cromwell's victories over the supporters of Charles II, the Scottish Guards were disbanded. However, they were reformed only ten years later, after Charles II was restored to the English and Scottish thrones. Now known as the Scottish Regiment of Foot Guards, it was later transferred (1686) to the establishment of the English Army and thus became part of the English Royal Guard, albeit being a Scottish corps. In 1712, after England and Scotland had been united into a single state in 1707, the Scots Guards were given their final denomination of the 3rd Regiment of Foot Guards.

At the beginning of the Napoleonic Wars, the three regiments of Foot Guards had a different internal composition: the 1st Regiment comprised three battalions and was larger than the other two, which had only two battalions each. The Grenadier

to take part in the British offensive launched against the Netherlands during 1799. After Napoleon became master of France, the various battalions of the Foot Guards served on several different fronts, always distinguishing themselves for their excellent discipline and training.

The 1st Battalion of the Grenadier Guards was sent to Sicily in 1806 in order to oppose the invasion of the island attempted by the French and their Neapolitan allies; in 1808, for just a few months, the battalion was sent to the Iberian Peninsula to defend Portugal. During the following year, it was dispatched to Walcheren in the Netherlands as part of the British expeditionary force that tried (with little success) to open a second front in Flanders while Napoleon was with the bulk of his army fighting the Austrian Empire. In 1812, the battalion went back to Spain, where it took part in the final phase of the Peninsular War that ended with the occupation of southern France in 1814. The 2nd Battalion of the Grenadier Guards was sent to the Iberian peninsula in 1810 and later participated in the military operations conducted by the British Army in the Netherlands during 1814. In 1815, the unit fought with great distinction in the decisive Battle of Waterloo. The 3rd Battalion of the Grenadier Guards took part in the failed Anglo-Russian invasion of the Netherlands that was launched in 1799, and was later sent to Sicily during 1806. In 1808 and 1809, it fought in the Iberian Peninsula, before being transferred to Walcheren in the Netherlands. In 1811, the battalion was sent again to Spain, where it fought until the end of the Peninsular War in 1814. During the following year, it participated with distinction in the Waterloo campaign.

The 1st Battalion of the Coldstream Guards took part in the Dutch campaign of 1799 as well as the Egyptian one of the following year, while from 1809–14 it fought with enormous courage in the Iberian Peninsula and southern France. The 2nd Battalion of the Coldstream Guards sent its light companies to Walcheren in 1809 and later to Spain during the following year; in 1815, the whole unit fought during the campaign which culminated at Waterloo. The 1st Battalion of the Scots Guards was sent to the Netherlands in 1799 and to Egypt during the following year; in 1809, it went to the Iberian Peninsula, serving under Wellington until 1814. The 2nd Battalion of the Scots Guards participated in the 1809 invasion of the Netherlands with its flank companies; during the following year, it sent three companies to the Iberian Peninsula. In 1814, it took part in the military operations conducted by the British Army in the Netherlands, while in 1815, the battalion fought at the Battle of Waterloo.

As is made clear by the above *excursus*, the Foot Guard regiments of the British Army took part in all the most important military operations conducted by Britain during the Napoleonic Wars. They were not merely 'parade' bodyguard corps but proper combatant units, whose level of professionalism was unrivalled in Europe. The

The Foot Guards 7

Grenadier of the 2nd Foot Guards, 1815. He is wearing the fur cap introduced for grenadiers in 1802, and has the shoulder wings that were distinctive of flank companies.

backbone of the three regiments was represented by the NCOs, professional soldiers who were able to train their men in the best possible way. It was their duty to transform young recruits into battle-hardened veterans, by preserving the traditions of their regiment. Obedience, endurance, loyalty and pride were the four key factors behind the elite status of the foot guardsmen. Uniforms and equipment always had to be in perfect order and completely clean, especially when performing guard duties at Windsor or at St James' Palace. Most of the common soldiers serving in the Foot Guard regiments came from the militia, and thus already had some experience of military life. Under guidance from the NCOs, however, they rapidly turned into professionals who were able to face any combat situation. Even more important than the NCOs, however, were the officers, who provided the Foot Guard regiments with their real and distinctive character. Most of these officers came from important aristocratic families of landowners, which had long military traditions. They were known as 'Gentlemen's Sons', and Wellington called them 'fellows in silk stockings', yet despite such nicknames, they showed on most occasions that their military competence was unrivalled and that they were not lacking courage. Buying an officer's commission in the guard infantry regiments was extremely costly, meaning that only the young sons of the aristocracy or the upper middle class could afford to do this. Daily life, in time of peace, was very expensive for such officers: it was spent in the most prestigious gentlemen's clubs of London and obliged the 'fellows in silk stockings' to invest large sums of money in order to have the most elegant uniforms and be part of 'high society'. All the officers of the Foot Guard regiments were extremely loyal to the Royal Family and considered Republican France to be a great potential menace for the social order of their own country; as a result, they were among the strongest supporters of the anti-French wars during the period here taken into account.

Chapter 2

The Line Infantry

During the Napoleonic period, the British line infantry maintained its internal organization prescribed by the 1792 regulations, without significant changes. It consisted of regiments with one or two battalions each, the latter being structured on ten companies. Each single battalion had its own headquarters, which consisted of the following elements: one lieutenant colonel, two majors, one adjutant, one surgeon, two assistant-surgeons, one quartermaster, one sergeant major, one staff sergeant paymaster, one sergeant armourer, one drum major, one corporal pioneer and ten pioneers. Each of these had precise administrative/combat functions, and their role was fundamental for the correct functioning of the battalion. The eleven pioneers, in particular, were to act as sappers or combat engineers, and thus had to open the way for their unit during marches or on the field of battle. Their main task was that of removing all the obstacles that their comrades could encounter during an operation, especially when the battalion was moving on broken terrain covered by trees or defensive structures built by the enemy. In addition to the headquarters company, there were the ten companies: eight battalion or centre ones made up of fusiliers, one right flank company of grenadiers and one left flank company of light infantrymen. Each company consisted of the following elements: one captain, two lieutenants or ensigns, two sergeants, three corporals, one drummer, one fifer and ninety privates. On paper, each battalion should deploy 1,000 soldiers, but the effective average strength varied from less than 500 men to a maximum of 800. The eight centre companies were numbered from '1' to '8' and could be assembled into four 'grand divisions' of two companies each. They could be divided into sixteen 'sub divisions' (also known as half-companies) or thirty-two sections; each half-company was to have fifty soldiers, while each section had just twenty-five men. In 1785, after the end of the American Revolution, the British line infantry was reduced to seventy-seven regiments, most of which had just one battalion each. With the beginning of the wars with Revolutionary France, it was greatly expanded from 1793 with the formation of many new regiments and the addition of second battalions to several of the existing units. At its maximum expansion, the British line infantry could deploy a total of 135 regiments.

What follows, for each of the units, is a brief organizational history for the years 1800–15. It should be noted that each regiment was numbered, but each unit also had its own specific denomination (frequently deriving from the surname of the colonel who had founded it or the name of the county where it had been created).

From left to right: grenadier of the 2nd Foot Guards, grenadier of the 1st Foot Guards and grenadier of the 3rd Foot Guards. All soldiers are wearing the parade dress that was used on service at the royal palace.

1st Regiment of Foot, 'The Royal Scots'
Raised in 1661, it had two battalions since 1686. A 3rd Battalion and 4th Battalion were added to the unit in 1804, this regiment being one of the few in the British line infantry to have four battalions.

2nd Regiment of Foot, 'The Queen's Royal'
Raised in 1661, it had two battalions since 1794. During 1796, the two battalions were merged into one.

3rd Regiment of Foot, 'The Buffs'
Raised in 1672, it had two battalions since 1803. The 2nd Battalion was disbanded in 1816.

4th Regiment of Foot, 'King's Own'
Raised in 1680, it received a 2nd Battalion and 3rd Battalion during 1799. The latter were disbanded in 1802, with the 2nd Battalion being re-raised in 1804 and disbanded again in 1815.

5th Regiment of Foot, 'Northumberland'
Raised in 1684, it had a 2nd Battalion during the years 1799–1803 and from 1804–16.

6th Regiment of Foot, '1st Warwickshire'
Raised in 1673, it had a 2nd Battalion during the period 1804–15.

7th Regiment of Foot, 'Royal Fusiliers'
Raised in 1685, it had a 2nd Battalion during the years 1795–96 and 1804–15.

8th Regiment of Foot, 'The King's'
Raised in 1685, it had a 2nd Battalion from 1804–15.

9th Regiment of Foot, 'East Norfolk'
Raised in 1685, it had a 2nd Battalion and 3rd Battalion between 1799 and 1802. The 2nd Battalion was re-raised in the period 1804–15.

10th Regiment of Foot, 'North Lincolnshire'
Raised in 1685, it had a 2nd Battalion during the years 1804–16.

11th Regiment of Foot, 'North Devonshire'
Raised in 1685, it had a 2nd Battalion from 1808.

12th Regiment of Foot, 'East Suffolk'
Raised in 1685, it had a 2nd Battalion from 1812.

13th Regiment of Foot, '1st Somersetshire'
Raised in 1685, it always had just a single battalion.

14th Regiment of Foot, 'Bedfordshire' ('Buckinghamshire' from 1809)
Raised in 1685, it had a 2nd Battalion during the period 1804–17 and a 3rd Battalion from 1813–16.

15th Regiment of Foot, 'Yorkshire East Riding'
Raised in 1685, it had a 2nd Battalion from 1799–1802 and during the years 1804–14.

16th Regiment of Foot, Buckinghamshire' ('Bedfordshire' from 1809)
Raised in 1688, it always had a single battalion.

17th Regiment of Foot, 'Leicestershire'
Raised in 1688, it had a 2nd Battalion between 1799 and 1802.

18th Regiment of Foot, 'The Royal Irish'
Raised in 1684, it had a 2nd Battalion from 1803–14.

19th Regiment of Foot, '1st Yorkshire North Riding'
Raised in 1689, it always had only a single battalion.

20th Regiment of Foot, 'East Devonshire'
Raised in 1688, it had a 2nd Battalion during the years 1799–1802.

21st Regiment of Foot, 'Royal North British Fusiliers'
Raised in 1678, it had a 2nd Battalion from 1804–16.

22nd Regiment of Foot, 'Cheshire'
Raised in 1688, it had a 2nd Battalion for some months during 1814.

23rd Regiment of Foot, 'Royal Welch Fusiliers'
Raised in 1689, it had a 2nd Battalion during the period 1804–14.

24th Regiment of Foot, '2nd Warwickshire'
Raised in 1689, it had a 2nd Battalion between 1804 and 1814.

25th Regiment of Foot, 'Sussex' ('King's Own Scottish Borderers' from 1805)
Raised in 1689, it had a 2nd Battalion and 3rd Battalion from 1795–96. A 2nd Battalion was re-raised from 1804–16.

26th Regiment of Foot, 'Cameronian'
Raised in 1689, it had a 2nd Battalion during the period 1804–14.

27th Regiment of Foot, 'Enniskillen'
Raised in 1689, it had a 2nd Battalion during years 1800–02 and 1804–17. A 3rd Battalion existed from 1805–16.

28th Regiment of Foot, 'North Gloucestershire'
Raised in 1694, it had a 2nd Battalion during the period 1803–14.

29th Regiment of Foot, 'Worcestershire'
Raised in 1702, it had a 2nd Battalion from 1795–96.

30th Regiment of Foot, 'Cambridgeshire'
Raised in 1702, it had a 2nd Battalion between 1803 and 1817.

31st Regiment of Foot, 'Huntingdonshire'
Raised in 1702, it had a 2nd Battalion during the period 1804–14.

32nd Regiment of Foot, 'Cornwall'
Raised in 1702, it had a 2nd Battalion during the years 1804–14.

33rd Regiment of Foot, '1st Yorkshire West Riding'
Raised in 1702, it always had just a single battalion.

34th Regiment of Foot, 'Cumberland'
Raised in 1702, it had a 2nd Battalion from 1805–17.

35th Regiment of Foot, 'Dorsetshire' ('Sussex' from 1805)
Raised in 1702, it had a 2nd Battalion from 1799–1803 and 1805–17.

36th Regiment of Foot, 'Herefordshire'
Raised in 1702, it had a 2nd Battalion during the period 1804–14.

37th Regiment of Foot, 'North Hampshire'
Raised in 1702, it had a 2nd Battalion during the years 1813–17.

38th Regiment of Foot, '1st Staffordshire'
Raised in 1705, it always had only one battalion.

39th Regiment of Foot, 'East Middlesex' ('Dorsetshire' from 1807)
Raised in 1702, it had a 2nd Battalion between 1803 and 1814.

40th Regiment of Foot, '2nd Somersetshire'
Raised in 1717, it had a 2nd Battalion from 1799–1802 and 1804–15.

41st Regiment of Foot, 'Royal Invalids'
Raised in 1719, it always had a single battalion.

42nd Regiment of Foot, 'Royal Highland'
Raised in 1739, it had a 2nd Battalion from 1803–14.

43rd Regiment of Foot, 'Monmouthshire'
Raised in 1741, it had a 2nd Battalion during the years 1804–17.

44th Regiment of Foot, 'East Essex'
Raised in 1741, it had a 2nd Battalion during the years 1803–16.

45th Regiment of Foot, '1st Nottinghamshire'
Raised in 1741, it had a 2nd Battalion between 1804 and 1814.

46th Regiment of Foot, 'South Devonshire'
Raised in 1741, it had a 2nd Battalion during the period 1800–02.

47th Regiment of Foot, 'Lancashire'
Raised in 1741, it had a 2nd Battalion from 1803–15.

48th Regiment of Foot, 'Northamptonshire'
Raised in 1741, it had a 2nd Battalion during the period 1803–14.

49th Regiment of Foot, 'Hertfordshire'
Raised in 1743, it had a 2nd Battalion from 1813–14.

50th Regiment of Foot, 'West Kent'
Raised in 1755, it had a 2nd Battalion during the period 1804–14.

51st Regiment of Foot, '2nd Yorkshire West Riding'
Raised in 1755, it always had only a single battalion.

52nd Regiment of Foot, 'Oxfordshire'
Raised in 1755, it had a 2nd Battalion from 1799–1803 and 1804–16.

53rd Regiment of Foot, 'Shropshire'
Raised in 1755, it had a 2nd Battalion during the period 1803–17.

54th Regiment of Foot, 'West Norfolk'
Raised in 1755, it had a 2nd Battalion during the years 1800–02.

55th Regiment of Foot, 'Westmoreland'
Raised in 1755, it always had a single battalion.

56th Regiment of Foot, 'West Essex'
Raised in 1755, it had a 2nd Battalion from 1804–16 and a 3rd Battalion between 1813 and 1814.

57th Regiment of Foot, 'West Middlesex'
Raised in 1755, it had a 2nd Battalion during the period 1803–15.

58th Regiment of Foot, 'Rutlandshire'
Raised in 1755, it had a 2nd Battalion from 1803–15.

59th Regiment of Foot, '2nd Nottinghamshire'
Raised in 1755, it had a 2nd Battalion between 1804 and 1816.

60th Regiment of Foot, 'Royal American'
Raised in 1755, it had four battalions until 1797, when a 5th Battalion was added, followed by a 6th Battalion in 1799. In 1813, another two battalions were added, for a total of eight. During the period 1816–19, the regiment was gradually reduced to just two battalions.

61st Regiment of Foot, 'South Gloucestershire'
Raised in 1756, it had a 2nd Battalion between 1803 and 1814.

62nd Regiment of Foot, 'Wiltshire'
Raised in 1756, it had a 2nd Battalion from 1799–1802 and 1804–16.

63rd Regiment of Foot, 'West Suffolk'
Raised in 1756, it had a 2nd Battalion between 1804 and 1814.

64th Regiment of Foot, '2nd Staffordshire'
Raised in 1756, it always had only one battalion.

65th Regiment of Foot, '2nd Yorkshire North Riding'
Raised in 1756, it always had a single battalion.

The ninety regiments can be divided into nine groups according to their date of birth: regiments 1–6 were raised following the Restoration of Charles II to the English throne; regiments 7–15 were created during the reorganization of the English Army carried out by James II around 1685; regiments 16–28 (although not all of them) were formed after the Glorious Revolution of William of Orange; regiments 29–41 were organized during the mobilization for the War of the Spanish Succession; regiments 42–49 were raised during the mobilization for the War of the Austrian Succession; regiments 50–70 were created due to the outbreak of the Seven Years' War; regiments 71–72 were organized due to the outbreak of the American Revolution; regiments 73–77 were formed for service in India; and regiments 78–90 were raised soon after the outbreak of hostilities with Revolutionary France. The seven infantry regiments organized during the 1780s were all employed during the Third Anglo–Mysore War of 1790–92, one of the greatest conflicts fought by Britain in India. Since the war was being carried on by the British East India Company and not by the British Crown, it was the former that paid for the expense deriving from the formation of these regiments (according to the Declaratory Act of 1788). When many European countries formed a military coalition to limit the territorial ambitions of Revolutionary France, Britain had no choice but to expand its military forces in view of the new campaigns that would have to be fought. This led to the creation of thirteen new infantry regiments, most of which were originally raised as volunteer units and later transformed into line corps. The patriotic response to the outbreak of a new war was incredible, and thus it was possible to enlarge the foot troops in a substantial way. During the period 1793–96, another forty-five infantry regiments (numbered 91–135) were recruited, all having a single battalion. These, however, had a very ephemeral history and had all been disbanded by the beginning of 1797. As a result, their progressive numbers were later given to new units, which had a much longer life. The following new regiments (numbered 91–104) were created during the period 1794–1815 and had a much more stable history:

91st Regiment of Foot, 'Argyllshire Highlanders'
Raised in 1794, it had a 2nd Battalion during the period 1804–15.

92nd Regiment of Foot, 'Gordon Highlanders'
Raised in 1794, it had a 2nd Battalion from 1803–14.

93rd Regiment of Foot, 'Sutherland Highlanders'
Raised in 1799, it had a 2nd Battalion between 1813 and 1815.

The Line Infantry 19

From left to right: grenadier of the 2nd Foot Guards, grenadier of the 1st Foot Guards, grenadier of the 3rd Foot Guards and two fusiliers of the 1st Foot Guards. All fur caps had a badge reproducing a flaming grenade on the back.

94th Regiment of Foot, 'Scotch Brigade'
Raised in 1794, it received a progressive number only in 1802. It always had just a single battalion.

95th Regiment of Foot, 'Rifles'
Raised in 1800, it had a 2nd Battalion from 1805 and a 3rd Battalion from 1809. The latter was disbanded in 1819.

96th Regiment of Foot
Raised in 1803, it had a 2nd Battalion from 1804.

97th Regiment of Foot, 'Queen's Own Germans'
Raised in 1798, it always had a single battalion.

98th Regiment of Foot
Raised in 1804, it always had only one battalion.

99th Regiment of Foot, 'Prince of Wales' Tipperary Regiment'
Raised in 1804, it always had a single battalion.

100th Regiment of Foot, 'Prince Regent's County of Dublin'
Raised in 1804, it always had just one battalion.

101st Regiment of Foot, 'Duke of York's Irish'
Raised in 1805, it always had a single battalion.

102nd Regiment of Foot
Raised in 1789 as the 'New South Wales Corps', it became a line regiment in 1808.

103rd Regiment of Foot
Raised in 1806 as a 'Royal Veteran Battalion', it became a line regiment in 1808.

104th Regiment of Foot
Raised in 1803 as the 'New Brunswick Fencibles', it became a line regiment in 1810.

Among the regiments listed above, the 94th had a very peculiar history: this, in fact, was a Scottish unit commanded by officers who had previously served as part of the Dutch Army's 'Scots Brigade'. Since the Eighty Years' War of 1568–1648, which secured the independence of the Netherlands from Spain, the Dutch Army had comprised a mixed Anglo–Scottish Brigade with three English regiments and three Scottish ones. During the Glorious Revolution of 1688, the Anglo–Scottish regiments of William of Orange followed him during his siezing of the English throne, after which the three English regiments became part of William's reformed English Army while the three Scottish ones went back to the Netherlands (assuming the denomination of the Scots Brigade). The latter corps took part in all the wars fought by the Dutch Army during the eighteenth century until 1782, when the ongoing Fourth Anglo–Dutch War caused great discontent among the Scots and forced the Dutch to transform the three regiments into Dutch ones. Most of the Scottish soldiers abandoned the Netherlands and joined the British Army, while several of their officers asked the British government to create a new Scots Brigade as part of the British Army. The officers' request was not accepted until the outbreak of war with Revolutionary France, when twenty-three of them were permitted to raise the new 94th Regiment of Foot, known as the 'Scotch Brigade'. The 97th Regiment, meanwhile, was recruited in Menorca from German-speaking prisoners of war from the Swiss regiments of the Spanish Army. Between 1796 and 1808, Spain was an ally of Revolutionary France and thus was at war against Britain. At that time, the Spanish Army comprised six mercenary infantry regiments made up of Swiss soldiers, from which the recruits for the 97th Regiment came. The last three regiments, numbered 102–104, were originally raised as different kinds of infantry units, and thus their history will be treated in the following chapters.

Considering the population of Britain, a general infantry establishment of over 100 regiments was very impressive for the standards of the Napoleonic Wars. Moreover, their large numbers were usually of high quality. Of all the 104 line infantry regiments listed in this chapter, ten were Irish units: the 18th Regiment of Foot ('Royal Irish'), 27th Regiment of Foot ('Enniskillen'), 83rd Regiment of Foot ('County of Dublin'), 86th Regiment of Foot ('Shropshire Volunteers'), 87th Regiment of Foot ('Prince of Wales' Irish'), 88th Regiment of Foot ('Connaught Rangers'), 89th Regiment of Foot, 99th Regiment of Foot ('Prince of Wales' Tipperary Regiment'), 100th Regiment of Foot ('Prince Regent's County of Dublin') and 101st Regiment of Foot ('Duke of York's Irish'). Of these, some had a remarkable history, such as the 'Royal Irish' or the 'Enniskillen'. The 'Royal Irish' was raised in 1684 by assembling together several independent garrison companies that existed in Ireland. During the Glorious Revolution, it supported William of Orange and thus was not disbanded like all the other existing Irish units. As a result, it was the oldest of the Irish regiments serving in the British Army. The 'Enniskillen' was raised in 1689 as a local militia unit, recruited from those Irishmen who supported William of Orange during his struggle against James II. The unit fought with great courage during the Williamite War in Ireland, and thereafter was made part of the English Army in 1690.

22 *Wellington's Infantry, 1805–1815*

Officer (left) and fusilier (right) of the 1st Foot Guards on campaign. Both figures are wearing the standard grey greatcoat used by the British infantry during winter.

Fusilier (left) and colour sergeant (right) of the 1st Foot Guards on campaign. They are wearing their grey greatcoats and using protective covers for their shakos.

Officer of the 2nd Regiment of Foot. He is wearing the standard black bicorn and red waist-sash that were employed by all officers.

(Black Watch) took part in all the most important military campaigns fought by the British Army, including the Seven Years' War (in North America) and the American Revolutionary War. During the Napoleonic Wars, the 1st Battalion of the regiment fought in the following campaigns: Egypt, 1801; Peninsula, 1808; Walcheren, 1809; Peninsula, 1812–14; and Waterloo, 1815. The 2nd Battalion, meanwhile, fought in the Peninsula between 1810 and 1812.

The 1st Battalion of the 71st Regiment of Foot participated in the following campaigns: Cape of Good Hope (South Africa) and La Plata (Argentina), 1806; Peninsula, 1808; Walcheren, 1809; Peninsula, 1810–14; and Waterloo, 1815. The 2nd Battalion remained on garrison duty in Britain. The 1st Battalion of the 72nd Regiment of Foot remained on garrison duty in South Africa for most of the Napoleonic period, while the 2nd Battalion remained in Ireland during the period taken into account. The 1st Battalion of the 73rd Regiment of Foot garrisoned New South Wales from 1809, while the 2nd Battalion fought in the Netherlands (1814) and at Waterloo (1815). The 74 Regiment of Foot served at Walcheren (1809) and in the Peninsular War (1811–14). The 75th Regiment of Foot was stationed in Sicily during the years 1811–14. The 1st Battalion of the 78th Regiment of Foot took part in the British occupation of Java from 1811–16, while the 2nd Battalion fought in Sicily (1806) and at Walcheren (1809) before participating in the Waterloo campaign of 1815. The 79th Regiment of Foot participated in the Egyptian campaign of 1801 and the Danish one of 1807, before fighting in the Peninsula (1810–14) and at Waterloo (1815). The 1st Battalion of the 91st Regiment of Foot was sent to Walcheren in 1809 and then to the Peninsula (1812–14); it later took part in the Waterloo campaign of 1815. The 2nd Battalion, meanwhile, was in the Netherlands during the campaign of 1814. The 1st Battalion of the 92nd Regiment of Foot participated in the Egyptian campaign in 1801 and the Danish one of 1807; later it was sent to Walcheren (1809) and the Peninsula (1810–14), before fighting at Waterloo. The 2nd Battalion of this unit remained in Ireland. The 93rd Regiment of Foot was stationed in South Africa until 1814, before being sent to North America in 1815 to fight at New Orleans.

Generally speaking, the Highlanders were excellent soldiers. They could be less disciplined than their English compatriots, but their courage and fitness were unrivalled. They would defend a position to the last man and were extremely proud of their regimental traditions. On many occasions, they were able to achieve success despite being in clear numerical inferiority, and their morale was usually very high. The Highlanders were used to existing in poor and rocky countryside, where living conditions were extremely harsh. Consequently, they could endure hardships of any kind while on campaign and could live for days with very little food. These mountaineers were able to move very rapidly on every kind of terrain, and thus had excellent skirmishing abilities. In combat, the Highlanders were prone to use their bayonets much more frequently than the English regiments, since their fighting spirit

28   *Wellington's Infantry, 1805–1815*

Colour sergeant of the 2nd Regiment of Foot. Thanks to the absence of shoulder wings, we know that this NCO is from a fusilier company.

was still that of the ancient Celtic warriors. When needed, however, they could deliver very accurate fire upon the enemy ranks. From an organizational point of view, the Scottish regiments had exactly the same structure as the English ones; their musicians, however, played bagpipes instead of fifes.

Chapter 4

The Light Infantry

During the first seventy years of the eighteenth century, the line infantry was the most important component of the European armies, since it made up the bulk of the troops mobilized by the various nations and had acquired a certain tactical superiority over cavalry. Highly trained and well-disciplined, it consisted of fusiliers who were able to march and manoeuvre in perfect order by maintaining shoulder-to-shoulder close formations. While moving on the battlefield, the line infantrymen advanced in columns; when stopping to open fire upon the enemy, they were deployed into long lines. After some rolling volleys of musketry were exchanged between the two opposing infantry formations, a clash could continue in two different ways: on most occasions, one of the two lines was shattered by the enemy fire and thus decided to retreat (usually keeping order among the ranks and readopting column formation); on some occasions, instead, it was necessary to fight hand-to-hand with bayonets to determine the outcome of the confrontation. Keeping order in the formations and delivering a regular fire were the key factors behind victory; as a result, training was absolutely decisive in transforming line infantry into an effective tactical tool. Generally speaking, battles were extremely static, since maintaining perfect order in the formations obliged the infantrymen to move very slowly. The transition from the column formation to the line was extremely delicate, since it exposed the fusiliers to sudden charges by cavalry. When confronting horsemen, line infantry usually adopted a standard defensive formation known as the square: this was another kind of close order, created to stop enemy attacks by using the bayonets as 'pikes' against mounted troops.

These formations and tactics were determined by the performance of the muskets that were used during the eighteenth century; flintlock weapons, whose loading operations were quite complicated. This meant that only one or two bullets were fired per minute, and even then only by line infantryman with good training. In addition, the flintlock muskets of this period were all smoothbores and thus were extremely inaccurate: when a bullet was fired, it came out from the weapon without a precise direction, since there were no grooves inside the barrel that could guide it. A flintlock musket was of some use only when fired up to a maximum of 200 metres from the target; as a result, during a battle, the line infantry formations had to come very close in order to use their weapons at all effectively. The muskets of this age were also extremely heavy, which

30   Wellington's Infantry, 1805–1815

Officer of the 3rd Regiment of Foot. The lapels of the uniform are folded back, a practice that was of common use, especially among officers of the light infantry regiments.

greatly limited the mobility of the foot soldiers. When moving on broken terrain, for example covered with rocks or with trees, it was practically impossible for them to keep the close formations in order. All the main tactical formations had been created for an ideal battlefield, consisting of a large plain where the opposing infantry could move without encountering obstacles. In this military system, soldiers were not required to think and act in an autonomous way: they only had to move as clockwork toys in order to put into practice the orders received. There was no space for initiative, and each infraction of discipline was immediately and harshly punished. The evolutions required on the battlefield were repeated every day during training sessions, under the incessant beat of the drums.

A perfect example of this kind of eighteenth-century war was the Prussian Army of Frederick the Great, which perfected close-order infantry tactics and was admired by all the officer corps of Europe. Frederick's infantrymen were the best of their time, and their methods of training were copied by all contemporary armies, whether enemies or allies. During the War of the Austrian Succession (1740–48) and the Seven Years' War (1756–63), however, several episodes showed that the Prussian line infantry was not as perfect as it may seem. It became apparent that it could experience serious problems while operating on broken terrain and when fighting against enemy units that employed 'hit-and-run' guerrilla tactics. In particular, the Prussians struggled to contend with the efficient light troops deployed by the Austrian Empire: these consisted of semi-regular light infantrymen, recruited from the inhabitants of the Balkans.

The light infantrymen of the Austrian Army had been fighting for decades against the Ottoman Turks on the southern frontier of the Austrian Empire. The adversaries lived in a state of endless conflict, during which both sides typically launched rapid incursions into the territory of their enemy to raid and pillage. Gradually, the Austrian frontier soldiers had learned to fight like their enemies, becoming expert in the art of skirmishing and scouting. Their usual area of operations was covered by mountains and woods, where each soldier had to move singularly rather than in column or line formation. Most of these soldiers were excellent huntsmen in their civilian life and were also farmers, living on the Balkan frontier as military settlers. Their innovative tactics derived from hunting and were based on the principle of 'open formation'. Each soldier was to advance independently, but keeping contact with the other members of his unit, thereby covering his advance behind the obstacles of the terrain (such as a tree, for example) and firing upon the enemy from a favourable position. The Austrian light infantrymen caused serious problems and losses to Frederick the Great's perfect line infantry on several occasions, thus creating a great impression around Europe. Although initially they were considered as simple murderers by the most traditionalist of their enemies, during the course of the Seven Years' War it became apparent that they could play a very important role on the battlefield. The other great powers of Europe, unlike Austria, could not count on a militarized border from which expert light fighters could be recruited. Consequently, they started to create their own light infantry corps from the best hunters and gamekeepers of their communities, and these new units soon assumed the denomination of Chasseurs or Jägers, meaning – in French and German respectively – 'huntsmen'. The members of these corps were usually dressed in green, like most of the contemporary civilian hunters, and similarly communicated with horns and not with drums like the line infantry. During the Seven Years' War, dozens of new light corps were raised in France and Prussia, following the Austrian example, showing similar efficiency on campaign and confirming that a new branch of the infantry had been born.

The conflict of 1756–63 was also fought in the Americas, with the clash between the British and French colonies located in the northern part of the New World. In North America, however, the tactical situation of the armies was completely different from that of Europe, with some form of 'local' light infantry having already existed for the past century. The terrain of the thirteen British colonies, as well as that of French Canada (New France), was mostly covered with dense forests and inhabited by native communities whose warriors all fought as lightly armed and highly mobile skirmishers. Colonial warfare consisted of rapid raids and incursions launched across the frontier, exactly as on the southern border of the Austrian Empire. As a result, each British or French colonist/farmer was also a militiaman with great skirmishing capabilities. In order to survive, each settler had to learn to hunt in the forests and fight against the natives by using the same methods. In the late seventeenth century, the first great war in the history of Colonial America was fought between English colonists and the native tribes. This conflict is commonly known as King Philip's War, from the nickname that the colonists gave to their main native opponent (a great leader whose actual name was Metacomet). The war consisted of a great native insurgency that took place on the borders of the English colonies from 1675–76, which almost lead to the expulsion of the colonists from that part of North America. By using their hit-and-run guerrilla tactics, the native warriors of Metacomet inflicted many losses on the colonial militia and destroyed a large number of English settlements. Learning from experience, however, the colonial authorities understood that it was necessary to create a light infantry corps that could oppose the native attacks by using the same tactics. Command of this new experimental unit was given to Benjamin Church, a settler with great combat experience in the woods; members of the new corps, consisting of a single company, came to be known as 'rangers'. During the second half of the conflict, Church's men obtained a series of victories over the natives and finally killed Metacomet during a skirmish in the woods. Indeed, the rangers proved a key factor in the final victory of the colonists.

The Light Infantry 33

Corporal of the 3rd Regiment of Foot. As is clear from the colour of the plume, he is from a fusilier company. The nickname of this unit ('The Buffs') derived from its regimental colour.

38 *Wellington's Infantry, 1805–1815*

Grenadier of the 6th Regiment of Foot (left) and fusilier of the 23rd Regiment of Foot (right). Fur caps were worn very rarely by the grenadier companies, usually only on parade.

from German recruits. Finally, another two battalions were raised during 1813 for service in the Americas during the War of 1812 against the United States. These last two battalions were recruited from German and Swiss prisoners of war who had been part of Napoleon's military forces.

As is clear from the above, the 60th Regiment of Foot continued to be strongly linked to the Americas during the Napoleonic Wars and remained the British foot regiment with the highest percentage of German/Swiss rankers. Of the eight battalions, only the 5th was entirely armed with rifles; the original four battalions had just one company equipped with rifled carbines, as did the 6th Battalion, while the last two battalions had two rifle companies each. From 1797, rifle units of the British light infantry started to be dressed in dark green, and thus this colour was worn by the entire 5th Battalion and by the rifle companies of the other battalions. The remaining companies, armed with smoothbores, continued to wear the standard red uniforms. The 1st Battalion was in Canada until 1798; it was later transferred to the West Indies (Jamaica) before being sent to South Africa in 1811. The 2nd Battalion remained in Canada until 1800, being transferred to the West Indies, where it remained for the entire Napoleonic Wars. The 3rd Battalion was in the West Indies from 1793–1815, while the 4th Battalion remained in the Caribbean except for a brief period from 1806–08 that was spent in South Africa. The 5th Battalion served in Ireland until 1799, when it absorbed the soldiers of a German mercenary regiment (Lowenstein's Chasseurs) that had been recently disbanded. From 1800–06 it was in the Americas, before being sent to the Iberian Peninsula, where it fought between 1808 and 1814. The 6th Battalion was always stationed in Jamaica, while the 7th Battalion existed only for a few years and remained in Canada. The 8th Battalion had a very short life, spent in Gibraltar as a garrison unit.

During the American Revolution, the British Army had to face the American 'minutemen', the militiamen of the Thirteen Colonies who were able to assemble their companies and fight in just one minute if needed. These irregular fighters were all armed with rifled muskets, the 'Kentucky rifles', and were skilled skirmishers: they were excellent marksmen and experts at concealing themselves in the woods. They caused serious problems for the British line infantry, especially during the first phase of the conflict, always avoiding fighting in the open field and being able to move much more rapidly than their British opponents. In 1758, each British line battalion had been ordered to train one of its companies as light infantry, but this measure was abolished with the end of the Seven Years' War. In 1771, a single light company was reintroduced in all the line battalions, but this measure had not yet been properly implemented when the conflict in the Thirteen Colonies began. As a result, to counter the minutemen, the British had to rely almost entirely on the ranger and light corps organized by the American loyalists. In addition, the British Army could also employ its Highland regiments as light infantry units, since these Scottish troops frequently had all the characteristics of excellent light infantrymen despite being line ones. With the end of the bloody American conflict, all the loyalist light corps were disbanded, together with the 'temporary' battalions that had been formed by assembling together light companies from different regiments.

The British infantry was greatly reduced in its numbers, but the lessons learned about light infantry fighting were not completely forgotten. One light company

Colour sergeant (left) and ensign (right) of the 9th Regiment of Foot. The spontoon was used specifically to defend the regiment's colours from enemy cavalrymen.

was retained in all the battalions, and this was confirmed by the new organizational regulations that were implemented in 1792. Nevertheless, the British light infantry still had many limits. First of all, its soldiers were still armed with flintlock smoothbores. In addition, the prejudices of the most traditionalist officers towards light infantry were still quite strong. As a result, during the Revolutionary Wars with France the

British Army had to rely on the recruiting of foreign and mercenary regiments from continental Europe in order to have enough light infantrymen. We will analyse these units in one of the following chapters, but it is important to remember that they were usually short-lived and were never considered a significant component of the British military forces. This situation changed only with the progression of the Revolutionary Wars, during which the French light infantry showed its mastery on several occasions. The British finally understood that a general reform was urgently needed if their army wanted to face the French chasseurs on anything like equal terms. The first step in this direction was taken in 1798, when the Duke of York – commander-in-chief of the British Army – authorized the publication of the *Regulations for the Exercise of Riflemen and Light Infantry*. These were written by the commander of the 60th Regiment of Foot's 5th Battalion and were the first manual for light infantry of the British Army. Their publication marked the beginning of an important debate that took place inside the officer corps. Some officers, the most traditionalist ones, did not want to create new independent regiments of light infantry and still considered the formation of temporary light battalions as the best way to have light corps when needed; other officers, the most innovative ones, wanted to select the fittest and most intelligent officers/rankers from all the existing line regiments in order to create new light infantry units. The latter position eventually prevailed, partly because the victories of Revolutionary France had isolated Britain from the rest of Europe and thus made the recruiting of mercenary light infantrymen from the continent virtually impossible.

Consequently, in January 1800, each of the following line regiments was required to send one captain, one lieutenant, one ensign, two sergeants, one corporal and thirty of its best privates to be trained as riflemen: 1st Foot (2nd Battalion), 21st Foot, 23rd Foot, 25th Foot, 27th Foot, 29th Foot, 49th Foot, 69th Foot, 71st Foot, 72nd Foot, 79th Foot, 85th Foot and 92nd Foot. The chosen men, who were the best marksmen of their respective units, made up a new independent corps of riflemen. It is interesting to note that half of the selected regiments were Scottish ones, since they already had a sort of light infantry status and were famous for the hardiness of their men. The initial idea by the Duke of York was to train these elite soldiers as riflemen and send them back to their original units in order to act as the core for the formation of rifle companies in each line regiment. The temporary training unit that had just been created was named the Experimental Corps of Riflemen and was commanded by Colonel Coote Manningham (one of the most expert light infantry officers in the British Army). He trained the riflemen by following his highly innovative ideas, which were published in 1800 as the *Regulations for the Rifle Corps formed at Blachington Barracks under the command of Colonel Manningham*. The members of the Experimental Corps of Riflemen dispensed with rigid and unthinking obedience to orders received, in order to be more

42 *Wellington's Infantry, 1805–1815*

Drummer of the 9th Regiment of Foot. All musicians wore shoulder wings on their uniforms as a mark of distinction.

autonomous on the battlefield and create a special relationship based on mutual trust with their officers and NCOs. A new sense of comradeship was strongly developed, with one 'soldier of merit' selected in each half-platoon to assume command of his squad when NCOs were absent and be in a privileged position to be promoted as corporal.

In total, the Experimental Corps of Riflemen comprised just five companies, each of which was divided into two equally sized platoons, which were in turn divided into four squads. The members of each squad trained and lived together every day, in order to develop a special personal relationship that would be of great use on the battlefield. Meritocracy was encouraged by every possible method, including prizes offered by the officers to the best marksmen under their command. Training of the new experimental corps was very intensive, comprising field exercises that were made as realistic as possible. The basic idea was to forge soldiers who would be able to think in an autonomous way and act very rapidly according to circumstances. Individual capabilities were fundamental in this regard, and thus only the best soldiers in the British infantry were admitted into the ranks of the Experimental Corps of Riflemen. Training included moving swiftly on broken terrain, surviving with only the few food resources that an enemy countryside could offer, skirmishing in the open field, penetrating the enemy's lines without being noticed, launching surprise attacks to occupy enemy outposts, scouting for larger units during an advance and acting as rearguard to cover a retreat. From the outset, the new riflemen were given dark green uniforms and black leather equipment.

In August 1800, after just a few months of effective training, three companies of the Experimental Corps of Riflemen joined an amphibious expedition launched against the Spanish arsenal of Ferrol. Although this mission ended in failure for the British Army, during the operations the companies of riflemen fought with great competence and covered the retreat of the line infantry. After the return of the three companies that had fought in Spain, new recruits were added to the newly christened Rifle Corps (the title being introduced in October 1800). These men, who mostly came from Fencible or Volunteer regiments, enabled the unit to be expanded and become a battalion. In February 1801, the battalion was transferred to the official establishment of the infantry and thus became a permanent unit. Then in 1802, it was officially transformed into a regiment and received the denomination of the 95th 'Rifle' Regiment. During subsequent years, the riflemen took part in all the most important campaigns fought by the British Army, always distinguishing themselves and winning an impressive number of battle honours. Due to their superior training and morale, they were usually employed as 'special forces' to accomplish missions that seemed impossible on paper. In 1805, a 2nd Battalion was added to the Rifle Regiment, followed by a

44 *Wellington's Infantry, 1805–1815*

Fusilier of the 11th Regiment of Foot. He is wearing the new 'Belgian' shako, which replaced the previous stovepipe model.

3rd Battalion in 1809. The two new units underwent the same training as the original one, and thus acquired its same special status; the only other unit of the British Army that was comparable to them in terms of quality was the 5th Battalion of the 60th Foot.

The 1st Battalion of the 95th Foot sent one of its companies to Denmark in 1801, and during 1805 it participated in the military operations taking place in Hanover, which had been occupied by Napoleon's troops. In 1807, five companies of the battalion participated in the ill-fated expedition to South America against Spanish-held territory in present-day Argentina and Uruguay; they were deemed essential in the British conquest of Montevideo, but were all captured during the subsequent assault against Buenos Aires. During 1808, all the ten companies were sent to the Iberian Peninsula, where they fought with enormous valour until 1814. Due to the heavy casualties suffered, the companies were reduced to eight in 1810, and then to just six in 1813. During that same year, one company fought in the operations in the Netherlands. In 1815, the entire battalion took part in the Belgian campaign and fought at Waterloo.

The 2nd Battalion, created from drafts chosen from line regiments as well as from militia volunteers, participated in the South American campaign of 1806–07 with three companies (that were all captured, like the rest of the British expeditionary force). In 1808, eight companies were sent to the Iberian Peninsula, before participating in the Walcheren campaign during the following year. Between 1810 and 1814, several companies of the battalion were sent to Spain and Portugal, while two participated in operations in the Netherlands in 1813 and 1814. Six companies took part in the Belgian campaign and fought at Waterloo, and the battalion was the first British unit to enter Paris after the defeat of Napoleon. The 3rd Battalion, meanwhile, created from drafts of the two existing battalions, participated with three companies in the Peninsular War during the years 1810–14. Two companies were sent to the Netherlands from 1813–14, while the remaining five participated in the War of 1812 against the United States, taking part in the disastrous Battle of New Orleans in 1815. Two companies of the battalion were also at the Battle of Waterloo.

The early success of the Rifles encouraged the British high command to implement its light infantry reforms by transforming several of the existing line regiments into light units. The main supporter of this process was General Sir John Moore, who was ordered by the Duke of York to retrain the 52nd Regiment of Foot and the 43rd Regiment of Foot as light units. Moore was commander of the 52nd Foot and had always been one of the officers who wished to expand the light component of the British infantry. During 1803, the two chosen regiments were transferred to the training camp of the Rifles at Shorncliffe in Kent, where they trained together with members of the 95th Regiment and were gradually transformed into light infantry corps. This change did not affect their internal structure, which continued to be based on battalions with

46 Wellington's Infantry, 1805–1815

Officer (left) and drummer (right) of the 26th Regiment of Foot. The drummer is wearing a jacket with reversed colours and a fur cap (the latter being quite popular on parade).

ten companies each, but did alter their tactics and combat doctrines. The new light infantrymen retained their red uniforms and continued to be armed with smoothbore muskets (albeit a special 'light' version), but learned how to fight in open order and act as skirmishers. From this moment onwards, the British Army started to include two distinct components of light foot troops: the elite Rifles, who were armed with rifled carbines and were mostly employed as 'special forces', and the light infantrymen of the converted regiments, who were equipped with smoothbore muskets but were trained as light skirmishers. The methods of training employed by Moore were very similar to those introduced by Manningham in 1800, which were based on the *Regulations for the Exercise of Riflemen and Light Infantry* published some time before by the commander of the 60th Regiment of Foot's 5th Battalion (the Swiss Baron de Rottenburg, a light infantry expert). From July 1803, the three units training at Shorncliffe were united together to form a Corps of Light Infantry commanded by Moore. In September 1805, the retraining of the 43rd Foot and 52nd Foot was completed and both units were later sent to the Iberian Peninsula. Here, together with most of the 95th Rifles and with some allied units, they formed a special Light Division that acted as Wellington's 'special corps'. The Light Division was structured on two brigades, comprising the following units:

1st Brigade
– 1st Battalion of the 43rd Regiment of Foot
– 1st Battalion of the 95th Rifle Regiment
– 3rd Battalion of the 95th Rifle Regiment (just five companies)
– 3rd Battalion of the Portuguese Caçadores

2nd Brigade
– 1st Battalion of the 52nd Regiment of Foot
– 2nd Battalion of the 95th Rifle Regiment
– 1st Battalion of the Portuguese 17th Line Infantry Regiment
– 2nd Battalion of the Portuguese 17th Line Infantry Regiment
– 1st Battalion of the Portuguese Caçadores

Following the operational success of the 43rd Foot and 52nd Foot, more line infantry units were transformed into light regiments during the Napoleonic Wars by undergoing new training sessions. By 1815, the following regiments of the British infantry had become light units (most of which were retrained by Baron de Rottenburg):

– 51st Regiment of Foot, transformed in 1809
– 68th Regiment of Foot, transformed in 1808
– 71st Regiment of Foot, transformed in 1809
– 85th Regiment of Foot, transformed in 1808
– 90th Regiment of Foot, transformed in 1815

As a result, by the end of the Napoleonic period, the British Army comprised the following light units: one regiment of rifles (with three battalions), one mixed regiment

Fusilier of the 26th Regiment of Foot. His headgear is a stovepipe shako, and he has the standard shoulder straps of centre companies on his jacket.

of rifles/light infantry (with eight battalions) and seven regiments of light infantry (former line units). These fought with great distinction during several campaigns, as shown by the following overview. The 43rd Foot had its 1st Battalion in Spain and Portugal from 1808–14; after disbandment of the Light Division, it participated in the Battle of New Orleans against the United States. The 2nd Battalion fought in Spain in 1808 and at Walcheren the following year. The 51st Foot took part in the Peninsular War from 1809 and continued to serve under Wellington until 1814, apart from a brief interruption during 1809, when it was sent to Walcheren. In 1815, it fought at Waterloo. The 52nd Foot had its 1st Battalion in Sicily during 1806 and 1807, then was sent to the Iberian Peninsula in 1809, where it remained until 1814. The unit also participated in the Battle of Waterloo. The 2nd Battalion was in Spain between 1808 and 1812, except for the brief interlude of the Walcheren campaign. In 1813–14, it participated in the military operations in the Netherlands. The 68th Foot was in Walcheren during 1809 and in Spain from 1812–14. The 1st Battalion of the 71st Foot took part in the Walcheren campaign of 1809 after a period of service in Spain; it was later sent again to the Iberian Peninsula, where it remained until 1814, before taking part at the Battle of Waterloo. The 2nd Battalion, however, always remained in Britain. The 85th Foot was in Walcheren before being dispatched to Spain, where it served during 1811 and 1813. In 1814 it went to North America and participated in the War of 1812 against the United States, taking part in the Battle of New Orleans in 1815. The 90th Foot only became a light regiment when the Belgian campaign of 1815 was already over.

Chapter 5

Royal Veteran Battalions and Fencible Regiments

Since 1688, the English Army had comprised a Corps of Invalids, made up of veteran soldiers who were no longer fit for active service but could still be employed for static/garrison duties. By the end of the eighteenth century, similar units existed in all the European armies and were sometimes called to serve during military conflicts. To become a member of the Corps of Invalids, a British veteran had to be chosen by the commissioners of the Royal Hospital in Chelsea. These commissioners analyzed the physical conditions of all the veterans who were no longer fit for active service and decided if these could be employed as garrison troops or could only receive a pension from the state. The Corps of Invalids was organized into a varying number of independent infantry companies, which were scattered across Britain in order to garrison several key points of the country. Thanks to the presence of the Invalids, a good number of 'active' military units could be freed from their garrison duties and thus be available for overseas service. Before the outbreak of the war with Revolutionary France, the Corps of Invalids comprised around 7,000 veterans, who usually served as garrison troops for a period of service of six years. In 1802, following the Peace of Amiens with France, it was decided to reorganize the Corps of Invalids and give to its units the new denomination of Royal Garrison Battalions. In 1804, the new and definitive denomination of Royal Veteran Battalions was introduced, but the functions and structure of the reorganized units were not changed. With the reform of 1802, the various independent companies of invalids were grouped together in order to form battalions, performing 'auxiliary' duties like working in depots or performing administrative functions. In addition, in case of foreign invasion, they would protect British territory as static defence corps. During the Napoleonic Wars, however, some battalions of veterans were also sent outside Britain and fought as auxiliary troops during various campaigns. The following units of the Royal Veteran Battalions, most of which had ten companies like the standard infantry battalions, were active during the period 1802–15:

1st Royal Veteran Battalion: This served in Portsmouth, Gibraltar, Holland, Landguard Fort (Suffolk) and Harwich before being disbanded in 1814.

2nd Royal Veteran Battalion: In 1806 a detachment from this unit was absorbed into the New South Wales Corps. The rest of the battalion served in Plymouth, Heligoland and Madeira until being disbanded in 1815.

3rd Royal Veteran Battalion: Raised on Jersey, it served as the garrison of this important British outpost until being disbanded in 1814.

4th Royal Veteran Battalion: Raised in Ireland, it also served in Gibraltar. In 1806, a detachment from this unit was absorbed into the New South Wales Corps. The battalion was disbanded in 1814.

5th Royal Veteran Battalion: This was formed in Guernsey and Alderney, where it served as the main garrison force until being disbanded in 1814.

6th Royal Veteran Battalion: The only unit to have an official denomination, the 'Royal North British'. It was raised in Scotland and served there until being disbanded in 1814.

7th Royal Veteran Battalion: Formed in Fulham, it was always based at the Tower of London. It was disbanded in 1814.

8th Royal Veteran Battalion: Organized in Fulham, it acted as the garrison of Fort Cumberland in Portsmouth and later of Heligoland. It was disbanded in 1815.

9th Royal Veteran Battalion: Differently from the previous units, which were all organized between 1802 and 1804, this was raised during 1805 in Edinburgh. It served as the garrison of Edinburgh Castle and sent one company each to the Orkney Isles and Shetland Isles. It was disbanded in 1814, except for the two 'detached' companies that continued to exist until 1815.

10th Royal Veteran Battalion: This was created in December 1806 on the Isle of Wight, with volunteers coming from the other veteran battalions. From the beginning, it was organized for service in Canada and not in Britain. Members of the unit were promised a grant of land in North America upon their retirement. When the War of 1812 between Great Britain and the United States broke out, the 10th Royal Veteran Battalion was one of the first units that had to fight for the defence of Canada. In April 1813, a small group of its members – just seventeen – were organized to form a Mounted Veterans Corps, charged with maintaining communications between the various defensive posts in the Montreal area. The battalion was disbanded in 1816.

11th Royal Veteran Battalion: Raised in 1807, it initially served on Guernsey. It was later sent to Bexhill, Winchelsea, the Isle of Man and Hythe. It was gradually disbanded during 1814 and 1815.

Lance corporal of the grenadier company, 48th Regiment of Foot. The presence of the fur cap and of an unusual white ammunition pouch indicates that this grenadier is dressed for parade.

English units
Cheshire Regiment, on ten companies, disbanded in 1801.
Devon and Cornwall Regiment, on ten companies, disbanded in 1801.
Loyal Durham Regiment, on ten companies, disbanded in 1801.
Loyal Essex Regiment, on ten companies, disbanded in 1801.
Loyal Nottingham Regiment, on ten companies, disbanded in 1801.
Loyal Somerset Regiment, on ten companies, disbanded in 1801.
Loyal Surrey Regiment of Rangers, on ten companies, disbanded in 1802.
Northampton Regiment, on ten companies, disbanded in 1801.
Northumberland Regiment, on ten companies, disbanded in 1801.
Prince of Wales' Leicester Regiment, on ten companies, disbanded in 1801.
Royal Lancashire Regiment, on ten companies, disbanded in 1801.
Scilly Company, disbanded in 1801.
Suffolk Regiment, on ten companies, disbanded in 1801.
York Regiment, on ten companies, disbanded in 1801.

Scottish units
1st Argyllshire Regiment, on ten companies, disbanded in 1799. (Highlanders)
2nd Argyllshire Regiment, on ten companies, disbanded in 1802. (Highlanders)
3rd Argyllshire Regiment, on ten companies, disbanded in 1802. (Highlanders)
Aberdeen Highland Regiment, on ten companies, disbanded in 1803. (Highlanders)
Angus Volunteers Regiment, on just two companies, disbanded in 1799. (Highlanders)
Angusshire Regiment, on ten companies, disbanded in 1802. (Lowlanders)
Breadalbane Regiment, on three battalions, disbanded in 1802. (Highlanders)
Caithness Legion, on ten companies, disbanded in 1802. (Highlanders)
Duke of York's Own Regiment, on ten companies, disbanded in 1802. (Highlanders)
Dumbarton Fencible Regiment, on ten companies, disbanded in 1802. (Highlanders)
Fifeshire Regiment, on ten companies, disbanded in 1803. (Lowlanders)
Fraser Regiment, on ten companies, disbanded in 1802. (Highlanders)
Glengarry Regiment, on ten companies, disbanded in 1802. (Highlanders)
Gordon Regiment, on ten companies, disbanded in 1799. (Highlanders)
Grant Regiment, on ten companies, disbanded in 1799. (Highlanders)
Lochaber Regiment, on ten companies, disbanded in 1802. (Highlanders)
Lord Elgin's Regiment, on ten companies, disbanded in 1802. (Highlanders)
Loyal British Regiment, on ten companies, disbanded in 1802. (Lowlanders)
Loyal Tarbent Regiment, on ten companies, disbanded in 1802. (Lowlanders)
Loyal Tay Regiment, on ten companies, disbanded in 1802. (Lowlanders)
North Lowland Regiment, on ten companies, disbanded in 1802. (Lowlanders)

Orkney Battalion, on three companies, disbanded in 1799. (Lowlanders)
Perthshire Highlanders, on ten companies, disbanded in 1799. (Highlanders)
Prince of Wales' Own Regiment, on ten companies, disbanded in 1802. (Lowlanders)
Princess Charlotte of Wales' Regiment, on ten companies, disbanded in 1799. (Highlanders)
Reay Highland Regiment, on ten companies, disbanded in 1802. (Highlanders)
Regiment of the Isles, on ten companies, disbanded in 1802. (Highlanders)
Ross and Cromarty Rangers, on ten companies, disbanded in 1802. (Highlanders)
Ross-Shire Highland Regiment, on just two companies, disbanded in 1799. (Highlanders)
Rothesay and Caithness Highlanders, on two battalions, disbanded in 1802. (Highlanders)
Royal Clan Alpine Regiment, on ten companies, disbanded in 1802. (Highlanders)
Royal Inverness Highlanders, on ten companies, disbanded in 1802. (Highlanders)
Shetland Battalion, on two companies, disbanded in 1802. (Lowlanders)
Southern Regiment, on ten companies, disbanded in 1799. (Lowlanders)
Sutherland Regiment, on ten companies, disbanded in 1799. (Highlanders)
West Lowland Regiment, on ten companies, disbanded in 1799. (Lowlanders)

Irish units
Ancient Irish Regiment, on ten companies, disbanded in 1802.
Loyal Irish Regiment, on two battalions, disbanded in 1802.
Loyal Limerick Regiment, on ten companies, disbanded in 1802.

Welsh units
Cambrian Rangers, on ten companies, disbanded in 1802.

Isle of Man
Royal Manx Regiment, on two battalions, disbanded in 1802. Re-raised on just four companies in 1803 and disbanded again in 1811.

Canada
New Brunswick Regiment, on six companies, disbanded in 1802.
Prince Edward Island Regiment, on two companies, disbanded in 1802.
Royal Canadian Volunteers, on two battalions, disbanded in 1802.
Royal Newfoundland Regiment, on ten companies, disbanded in 1802.
Royal Nova Scotia Regiment, on eight companies, disbanded in 1802.

The number of Scottish Fencible units was particularly high because in Scotland there were no militia units like in the rest of Britain, and thus a large number of men were available for home military service. Most of the Scottish Fencible Regiments were Highland ones. All Fencible units could be employed only on British territory; they could be sent to serve overseas only with the formal consent of their members. By 1802, all the British Fencible units had been disbanded, but in 1803, the Canadian ones were reorganized as follows:

Canadian Fencible Infantry, on ten companies, disbanded in 1816.
New Brunswick Fencible Infantry, on ten companies, became a line regiment during 1810.
Newfoundland Fencible Infantry, on ten companies, disbanded in 1816.
Nova Scotia Fencible Infantry, on ten companies, disbanded in 1816.

Chapter 6

The British Troops in Canada

When the USA gained its independence in 1783, Britain was able to retain possession of Canada. Indeed, Canada remained the largest colony of the British Crown, at a time when India was still administered by the private East India Company and Australia was only in the early phases of its colonization. From an administrative point of view, British Canada was divided as follows: Lower Canada, Upper Canada, Nova Scotia, New Brunswick, Newfoundland, Prince Edward Island and Cape Breton Island. The economies of all these territories had a precise role in the global commercial system created by Britain, and were mostly based on the fur trade and fishing. Exploitation of forests for wood was also a vital activity: during the long wars against Revolutionary and Napoleonic France, Canada became extremely important for Britain as a source of high quality wood for building warships. In general, the territory of Canada was not as economically developed as that of the USA, but its population (albeit being quite small) was made up of sturdy and courageous people. The troops garrisoning Canada between 1800 and 1815 comprised three different kinds: British regular units, Canadian militia units and Canadian volunteer units. The militia system of Canada derived from the French colonial period and remained extremely efficient under the British, as the US Army learned during its attempted invasion of Canada. In 1812, at the outbreak of the war with the USA, the British regular military units stationed in Canada were extremely scarce from a numerical point of view, consisting of just 6,034 men and including the following corps:

– 8th Regiment of Foot (1st Battalion in Canada, 2nd Battalion in Nova Scotia and New Brunswick)
– 41st Regiment of Foot
– 49th Regiment of Foot
– 100th Regiment of Foot
– Six companies of the 98th Regiment of Foot (in Nova Scotia)
– Four companies of the 99th Regiment of Foot (in Nova Scotia)
– 10th Royal Veteran Battalion
– Detachments of the Royal Artillery
– Detachments of the Royal Engineers

Colour sergeant of the 57th Regiment of Foot. Note the sash worn wrapped around the waist, which was distinctive of NCOs; the latter's central band was in the distinctive colour of each unit, except for regiments that had purple/red as a facing colour which had a white central band (in this picture the artist has inverted colours by mistake).

- Detachments of the Royal Military Artificers/Royal Sappers and Miners
- Canadian Fencible Infantry
- Nova Scotia Fencible Infantry
- New Brunswick Fencible Infantry
- Newfoundland Fencible Infantry

The core of the British troops in North America was represented by the 41st and 49th Regiments of Foot, which had been garrisoned in Canada for a long time: these two units had learned how to fight in the woods of North America and had a special relationship with the local population. The four Fencible units were also of good quality, despite having quite peculiar histories. The Canadian Fencible Infantry was originally raised in Scotland from Highlanders who were keen on emigrating to Canada. During 1803, however, some misunderstandings regarding the terms of enlistment led to the mutiny of the recruits before their departure from Scotland. As a result, only the commissioned officers of the unit and some NCOs were finally sent to North America in 1804, with orders to recruit the required rankers from the local colonists. Many of the Canadians who joined the unit were sons of 'Loyalists' who had abandoned the Thirteen Colonies after they became independent from Britain, and had settled in the southern areas of Canada. The Nova Scotia Fencible Infantry, as is clear from its name, was raised in Nova Scotia (a peninsula in eastern Canada), but was garrisoned in Newfoundland during the period 1805–12. The original New Brunswick Fencible Infantry was transformed into the 104th Regiment of Foot in 1810 after it volunteered for overseas service in 1808. To replace the original Fencible unit, another one having the same denomination and internal organization was raised in 1813 (which was disbanded, like all the other Canadian Fencibles, in 1816). The Newfoundland Fencible Infantry was mostly recruited from expert fishermen and boatmen living on Newfoundland Island; as a result, in 1812, five of its companies were sent to serve as marines on the Great Lakes. In addition to those listed above, the British forces in Canada also included another 'regular' unit, known as the French Independent Companies, which was raised in September 1812 by recruiting French deserters and prisoners of war, who were transferred from England to Canada. The corps comprised just two companies, which soon became infamous for their slack discipline, and had to act as a garrison unit for static defence. The French Independent Companies, which had dark green 'rifle' uniforms, were disbanded in early May 1814.

In Canada, just like in the USA, the militia was formed by all the able-bodied men who were eligible for military service according to their age. Since the foundation of the first French settlements in the early decades of the seventeenth century, the Canadians had to adopt a form of local military organization in order to repulse the violent raids of the various native tribes. This system was implemented during the eighteenth century and saw the Canadian militiamen fighting with great valour against the British and their native allies during the French–Indian War. Unlike what happened in the Thirteen Colonies, the militia units of French Canada were under quite strict control from the central authorities of the colony. Generally speaking, the Canadian militias had fewer men than their American equivalents, but their members were individuals with superior military capabilities. Most of the settlers living in Canada were huntsmen, and thus were used to travel long distances in the worst weather conditions. They had an excellent knowledge of the vast forests and plains surrounding them, and were all expert marksmen (employing long rifled muskets like the American colonists). Thanks to their mobility and great capacity to organize ambushes, the Canadian militiamen were able to fight against the natives on almost equal terms. Their knowledge of guerrilla warfare allowed them to launch surprise attacks very easily. Canada's militiamen, in addition, were ready to operate during the winter, and thus had all the necessary equipment to survive extremely cold temperatures. Rivers and lakes were no barriers for them, since the use of canoes was extremely common. In general, albeit quite few compared with their American opponents, the Canadian militia were excellent soldiers. The British inherited the militia system from the French and did nothing to change it. However, they tried to 'regularize' as much as possible the Canadian militia units in order to transform them into a proper auxiliary army that could support the regular forces. Most of Canada's population consisted of Francophone settlers, who had always been extremely loyal to France until the very last days of the French–Indian War. Consequently, at the outbreak of the War of 1812, the British authorities feared that these men could refuse to serve in the militia or revolt against the Crown. Nevertheless, the Canadian colonists all remained loyal to Britain, with no distinctions existing between French- and English-speakers. The Canadians already considered their territories to be a nation, and the foreign aggression of the USA did nothing else but strengthen their patriotic feelings. From 1791, administratively, Canada was divided into two provinces: Lower Canada and Upper Canada. In addition to these, there was the so-called 'Indian Territory' and the smaller Atlantic Colonies: the former comprised all the unsettled lands that were located west of the Great Lakes, while the latter were formed by the smaller British colonies that were situated on the Atlantic coast (Nova Scotia, New Brunswick, Newfoundland, Prince Edward Island and Cape Breton Island). For practical reasons, we will describe the organization of the Canadian militia and volunteers for each of the above territories.

The province of Lower Canada corresponded to the former territory of New France, and thus comprised most of the Francophone settlers in British North America. It had a much larger population than Upper Canada and comprised the three most important cities of British North America: Québec, Montréal and Trois-Rivières. The militia of this colony comprised an active force (known as the Select Militia) and a reserve one (the Sedentary Militia). The former, activated only in case of foreign menace, consisted of the best elements from the general Sedentary Militia. When a unit was called to serve, no matter whether from the Select Militia or Sedentary Militia, it received the further title of 'Embodied' (which meant it was attached to the regulars). In February 1812, as part of the mobilization for the war against the USA, a total of 6,500 militiamen were activated to form the Select Embodied Militia of Lower Canada. This was initially structured on four infantry battalions with 800 men each, which were to serve for a period of two years. After war was declared, a 5th Battalion was added on 21 September. In late June 1813, the flank companies of the five existing units were assembled together in order to form two independent battalions of light infantry, called Militia Light Infantry Battalions. These temporary units were dissolved on 25 November 1813, with the various companies returning to their original battalions. A 6th Battalion was formed on 28 February 1813 and briefly served as the garrison of Québec; this had a smaller establishment compared with the other battalions, and was disbanded in September 1814. In March 1814, the 5th Battalion was reorganized as an independent light infantry unit and received the denomination of Canadian Chasseurs (see below). The original four units continued to serve with distinction until the end of the war, being discharged only on 1 March 1815. During the War of 1812, the Select Militia of Lower Canada comprised the following units (which were all disbanded at the end of hostilities):

Canadian Voltigeurs: This unit was raised in April 1812, during the pre-war mobilization. It was an elite corps of light infantry, which soon became legendary because of its great achievements during the conflict. As clear from its denomination, it was entirely made up of French-speaking colonists and consisted of a single battalion with about 550 soldiers (assembled in eight companies). Curiously, attached to the corps there was also a company of native warriors who served as scouts. Dispersed in various small detachments that were attached to several major military units, the Voltigeurs Canadiens fought as scouts and skirmishers with enormous valour (especially during the early phases of the American invasion). The term '*voltigeur*' was used in the French Army to indicate elite light infantrymen; members of this Canadian unit were dressed and equipped as light skirmishers.

Frontier Light Infantry: This small corps consisted of just two companies and was created to patrol the American border south of Montréal. On 13 August 1813, after less than three months in existence, it was attached to the Canadian Voltigeurs, the Frontier Light Infantry units becoming the 9th and 10th Companies of the famous Francophone corps.

The British Troops in Canada

From left to right: officer of the 52nd Regiment of Foot, officer of the 87th Regiment of Foot, officer of the 9th Regiment of Foot, officer of the 73rd Regiment of Foot and officer of the 97th Regiment of Foot. Only two figures are wearing the lapels of their uniform folded back, in order to form a frontal plastron.

Canadian Chasseurs: As we have seen, this unit was the former 5th Battalion of the Select Embodied Militia. With its new denomination, it was usually brigaded with the Canadian Voltigeurs and Frontier Light Infantry. In total, the Canadian Chasseurs had just six companies.

Independent Company of Militia Volunteers: Created in May 1813, this unit was soon attached to the Frontier Light Infantry. Some months later, in February 1814, the Independent Company of Militia Volunteers was completely absorbed into the Frontier Light Infantry.

Corps of Canadian Voyageurs: This was a rather unusual corps raised by the North-West Fur Company, which operated in the vast areas located around Hudson Bay. The '*voyageurs*' were the Canadian equivalent of the American trappers, being frontier huntsmen who lived a very solitary life in the woods of North America. The Corps of Canadian Voyageurs comprised a number of employees of the North-West Fur Company. This unit was created in October 1812, with the main objective of militarizing the *voyageurs* and transforming them into proper soldiers. These men played a crucial role during the War of 1812, since their first responsibility was protecting the vital supplies which moved from the city of Montréal to the western outposts of the Indian Territory. On 14 March 1813, after becoming famous for the poor discipline of its members, the unit was finally disbanded.

Provincial Commissariat Voyageurs: This unit was formed on 8 April 1813 to act as a replacement for the recently disbanded Corps of Canadian Voyageurs. The new corps continued the activities of the previous one, but with a higher level of efficiency and discipline. It consisted of one captain, ten lieutenants, ten sergeants and 400 rankers.

Québec Volunteers: This unit was raised in Québec City in November 1812, being made up of a single infantry battalion with six companies. Initially, it was also to have an attached battery of artillery, but this was never formed. On 13 February 1813, the Québec Volunteers were absorbed into the new 6th Battalion of Select Embodied Militia.

Compagnie des Guides: This was a small cavalry unit, also known as the Corps of Guides. Formed in September 1812, it comprised just two officers and thirty troopers.

Canadian Light Dragoons: Recruited in Montréal District during the spring of 1813, this small cavalry corps comprised just eighty men (assembled into a single troop). The unit saw much action and took part in several engagements, being finally disbanded only in May 1815.

Dorchester Provincial Light Dragoons: Raised during the spring of 1813 like the Canadian Light Dragoons, this corps was also a small cavalry unit. It consisted of a single troop of sixty-eight men, who were armed and equipped by the government but had to buy horses and uniforms at their own expense. The Dorchester Provincial Light Dragoons served in Québec until being disbanded in March 1815.

Royal Militia Artillery: This consisted of just one officer and twenty-two gunners, who were detached from the urban militia of Montréal in September 1812 in order to be absorbed into the Select Embodied Militia.

Corps of Provincial Royal Artillery Drivers: Formed in April 1813, this small corps was attached to the regular detachments of the Royal Artillery that were operating in Montréal District. The Canadians had to provide drivers for the batteries of the regular artillery, since most of the British artillerymen were employed as gunners and not for auxiliary duties.

Since it was directly menaced by the American invasion, Lower Canada also mobilized its Sedentary Militia. This numbered some 54,000 militiamen, who were organized in two different ways according to their ethnic origins. The Sedentary Militia of the Francophone communities had the parish company as their basic unit: each parish (generally corresponding to a village) was to provide an infantry company commanded by a captain. The various parish companies were assembled into three divisions, which had more or less the same numerical establishment as a regiment. Each of the three districts that made up the province of Lower Canada (Québec, Montréal and Trois-Rivières) had one of these divisions. The few English-speaking settlers of Lower Canada had a different military organization: they lived in the so-called Eastern Townships, which had been settled by Loyalist colonists during the American Revolution, and thus formed an independent district. The Eastern Townships District had a militia that was organized according to counties, in perfect British style. Each county, according to its population, was to provide one or more infantry regiments with six battalions each. The single battalions could sometimes have an attached troop of cavalry. While this was generally the case in rural areas, in the major cities of Québec, Montréal and Trois-Rivières the situation was completely different. These important centres had several infantry battalions of urban militiamen. Québec had three infantry battalions: the 1st and 2nd were made up of Francophone citizens, while the 3rd one comprised Anglophone militiamen, Montréal also had three infantry battalions: the 1st was made up of English-speaking citizens, while the 2nd and 3rd comprised French-speaking militiamen. The urban militia of Trois-Rivières consisted of a single infantry battalion. Québec's battalions, created in 1803, had flank companies like those of the regular military forces; these were made up of chosen volunteers rather than ordinary militiamen. The battalions from Montréal had flank companies too, which were assembled for some time in order to form a temporary elite battalion. The urban militias of Québec and Montréal also comprised one troop of cavalry and two companies of artillery each, which were all formed of well-educated gentlemen/volunteers. The urban militias took part in no significant military actions during the War of 1812, and were disbanded as soon as the American menace vanished in 1815.

The province of Upper Canada had been mostly inhabited, at least initially, by Loyalist Americans who abandoned the Thirteen Colonies during the revolution against Britain. Much of the combat operations of the 1812–15 war took place on its territory, and it thus suffered greatly from the devastations caused by the battling armies. Despite having a smaller population than Lower Canada, Upper Canada made a significant contribution to the British war effort. From a geographical point of view, Upper Canada comprised the vast territory located between the western border of Québec province and the city of Windsor on Lake Huron. In total, the province embraced eight districts, which were divided into several counties. The Sedentary Militia of Upper Canada was much younger than that of Lower Canada, having been organized for the first time in 1793. Similarly to what happened in the Eastern Townships District of Lower Canada, it was based on county regiments of infantry that consisted of a single battalion with ten companies. In March 1812, some months before the outbreak of the war with the USA, each battalion was enlarged with the addition of two flank companies made up of volunteers, all aged under 40. On 18 March 1813, a single battalion of Select Embodied Militia with ten companies was formed in Upper Canada. In total it comprised around 500 men, being the best elements of the Sedentary Militia. The companies of this single battalion took part in several important engagements during the war and proved to be units of high quality (comparable to British regular units). The province of Upper Canada also deployed the following independent corps during the War of 1812 (which were all disbanded at the end of hostilities):

Glengarry Light Infantry: On 13 February 1812, even before the declaration of war, the Glengarry Light Infantry was raised from Catholic Scottish settlers who lived in eastern Upper Canada (Glengarry District). Since most of this battalion's members came from the same areas of Scotland, the Glengarry Light Infantry was characterised

From left to right: drum major, sapper and musicians of a line infantry regiment. The drum major of each regiment had the most extravagant uniform of his unit; in this case it comprises a bicorn with silver lace and a decorated crossbelt. Like for all musicians, the jacket is in reversed colours. The sapper wears a fur cap and has special personal equipment, comprising a protective leather apron and small leather bag. All sappers, like musicians, had shoulder wings.

by a strong esprit-de-corps that made it an elite unit. The 730 soldiers of this corps were organized into eight light companies, who all underwent intensive light infantry training and were dressed exactly like the famous Rifle Regiment of the regular British Army. The soldiers of this corps proved to be excellent marksmen and took part in many important actions of the war against the USA. The Glengarry Light Infantry was finally disbanded in 1816, having gained the deep respect of its enemies.

Caldwell's Rangers: Also known as the Western Rangers, this corps had two companies and was created in April 1813. Members of this unit were to serve side-by-side with the native allies of Britain in Upper Canada, and were equipped as proper light infantry rangers.

Volunteers of 1812: As we have seen, the infantry battalions of the Sedentary Militia were expanded with the creation of volunteer flank companies. In order to face the American invasion, however, the volunteers of Upper Canada also formed some independent corps that became known as the Volunteers of 1812. These were named after their county of origin and comprised six companies of rifles, ten troops of cavalry and three companies of artillery. In addition, there was one infantry company of freed black slaves, one company of naval infantry (formed for service on the Great Lakes) and one company of artillery drivers.

Loyal Kent Volunteers: A single company of volunteer militiamen, formed on 25 November 1813 in Kent County. It was later attached to the battalion of Select Embodied Militia.

Loyal London Volunteers: A single company of volunteer militiamen, formed on 24 November 1813 in the small town of London (Upper Canada). It was disbanded on 24 February 1814.

Loyal Essex Volunteers: A single company of volunteer militiamen, formed in March 1814 in Essex County. Also known as the Essex Rangers, it was disbanded on 24 March 1815.

Provincial Light Dragoons: These consisted of just three small corps, each formed in a different county of Upper Canada. The Niagara Provincial Light Dragoons were a troop of just fifty men, which was renamed as the Niagara Frontier Guides on 24 October 1814. The other two troops were created in April 1813 and later assembled into a single unit.

Incorporated Artillery Company: Raised in March 1813, it comprised both artillerymen and artillery drivers who were absorbed into the Select Embodied Militia.

Provincial Royal Artillery Drivers: Formed during January 1813, this small corps (two companies) was attached to the regular detachments of the Royal Artillery that were operating in Upper Canada. The local Canadians had to provide drivers for the batteries of the regular artillery, since most of the British artillerymen were employed as gunners and not for auxiliary duties.

Corps of Provincial Artificers: Formed in March 1813 to assist the regular Royal Engineers in Upper Canada, this unit was also known as the Coloured Corps because all its members were freed black slaves.

In 1812, the Indian Territory of Canada was mostly unsettled and was defended by just a few forts; as a result, very few military units were raised from it. The only inhabitants of the Indian Territory were *voyageurs* (hunters) and fur traders, who were partly 'regularized' in order to serve in proper military corps. Attacking from the upper Mississippi Valley, the British/Canadian forces were able to capture northern Michigan and Wisconsin from the Americans, and kept the initiative in this theatre of operations for most of the war. The first unit to be formed in the Indian Territory was the Michigan Fencibles, a small infantry company of just forty-five men that was created by recruiting *voyageurs* and fur traders. Like the other units of Fencibles, it was formed to garrison a specific area of territory, being stationed in the strategic position of Fort Mackinac. The corps was disbanded at the end of the conflict, on 28 June 1815. In July 1814, other Francophone *voyageurs* were recruited in the Indian Territory in order to form some volunteer companies: these became known as the Mississippi Volunteers and initially consisted of just one company with sixty-five men. Apparently, this volunteer corps also comprised a small detachment of artillery.

The general militia of Nova Scotia consisted of twenty-six infantry battalions, known by the name of the county in which they were formed. At the time, Nova Scotia had twelve counties, so each of them formed a number of infantry battalions according to its population. Some of the infantry battalions had attached artillery companies. In addition, since 1813, each of them had two additional companies (one of light infantry and one of rifles). During the conflict, a total of about 500 militiamen were embodied for active service, fearing naval incursions from the American fleet. The city of Halifax, the capital of Nova Scotia, also deployed one volunteer company of artillery. The general militia of New Brunswick was organized on county infantry battalions like that of Nova Scotia, albeit smaller. In December 1812, to replace the local garrison of regulars that was transferred to mainland Canada, 500 militiamen were embodied for active service. Saint John, the colony's capital, had one company of volunteer artillery. Newfoundland had no militia units, only a volunteer corps known as the Loyal Volunteers of Saint John, which comprised five infantry companies and was later renamed as the Saint John's Volunteer Rangers. It was disbanded during the summer of 1814. Prince Edward Island had three infantry regiments of the militia

Grenadier (left) and officer (right) of the 79th Highlanders. The soldier is wearing the pre-1796 coat of the British infantry, with separated frontal lapels in regimental colour. The officer is wearing the red sash on his left shoulder, as prescribed for officers of the Highland units.

Corporal of the 42nd Highlanders (left) and grenadier of the 92nd Highlanders (right). Both figures are from grenadier companies, as shown by their white plumes and shoulder wings.

and three volunteer infantry companies in its capital, the city of Charlottetown. Each militia regiment was formed in one of the three counties that made up the colony, and included a different number of battalions according to its population. The three volunteer companies of Charlottetown were named the Loyal Scottish Volunteers, Royal Kent and Prince's Regent Volunteers. On Cape Breton Island the local militia consisted of twenty infantry companies, each commanded by a captain and two lieutenants.

Chapter 7

The British Troops in the West Indies

By the end of the eighteenth century, the islands collectively known as the West Indies, located in the Caribbean, were one of the most profitable areas of the world from an economic point of view. Having long been colonized by the European powers, they produced large amounts of sugar that was sold around the globe at very high prices; in addition, albeit on a smaller scale, they produced some other very profitable crops like indigo and coffee. Several of these islands were colonies of Great Britain, and represented about one-third of the country's foreign trade. Thanks to the direct taxes and duties from the Caribbean colonies, Britain became the most important of the colonial powers during the eighteenth century. As a result, it was absolutely fundamental for the Crown to protect such a lucrative portion of the ever-expanding British Empire. This was particularly true when, with the outbreak of the Revolutionary Wars, the British West Indies started to be menaced by the French, who had their own flourishing colonies in the Caribbean. Operating in the West Indies, however, was difficult for the British Army: the local tropical climate was unsustainable for European troops, who were frequently decimated by terrible diseases such as the infamous 'tropical fevers'. Consequently, British soldiers preferred avoiding service in the West Indies due to the unhealthy local conditions.

To solve this problem and to garrison the Crown's possessions in that part of the world, the British Army had no choice but to raise an increasing number of military units from the local communities of free blacks. These were accustomed to the climate and temperatures of the Caribbean, and thus could easily live in that theatre of operations. Until 1793, the British military garrison of the West Indies had been entirely made up of white regular regiments, which were sent to the Caribbean for periods of service before being transferred to other areas of the empire. A single local unit existed, the Carolina Corps, which consisted of 300 American Loyalist black former slaves who had abandoned the Thirteen Colonies in 1779 and were resettled by the British authorities in the West Indies. Many of them came from the Carolinas, hence the unit's name. In October 1793, the first of several new black units was formed, the Corps of Black Military Artificers and Pioneers. Mostly recruited from ex-criminals who had been freed, it comprised 300 pioneers and 100 artificers. This unit was followed by several others, which usually had the denomination of 'rangers'

Officers of the 42nd Highlanders, wearing parade dress. Note the Kilmarnock bonnet with many ostrich feathers, that was typical of the later years of the period.

and a distinct light infantry nature. Many of these were originally raised by royalist French officers who had joined the British cause after the outbreak of the revolution; they usually consisted of 200–300 soldiers each, having some experience of jungle fighting. The ranger corps were soon supplemented by garrison units created for static defence, but all these early black units had a distinctive temporary character and only a semi-regular status. This chaotic situation came to an end in 1795, when the British authorities finally decided to raise some regular West India Regiments from the free blacks living in their Caribbean colonies. The first eight such units were created at this time, with white officers and NCOs. A single regiment consisted of one battalion, with ten companies (eight centre and two flank units). Recruitment was completed for all regiments by 1798, and the following units had been formed:

– 1st West India Regiment (Whyte's)
– 2nd West India Regiment (Myer's)
– 3rd West India Regiment (Keppel's), disbanded in 1819
– 4th West India Regiment (Nicolls'), disbanded in 1819
– 5th West India Regiment (Howe's), disbanded in 1817
– 6th West India Regiment (Whitelocke's), disbanded in 1817
– 7th West India Regiment (Lewes'), disbanded in 1802
– 8th West India Regiment (Skerret's), disbanded in 1802

These regiments proved to be excellent units, being employed with success against the French as well as to deal with slave uprisings. As a result, another four West India Regiments were recruited in 1798:

– 9th West India Regiment, renumbered as the 7th West India Regiment in 1802
– 10th West India Regiment, renumbered as the 8th West India Regiment in 1802
– 11th West India Regiment, disbanded in 1803
– 12th West India Regiment, disbanded in 1803

The West India Regiments absorbed all the existing temporary infantry units of free blacks, including the Carolina Corps. In order to maintain the original establishments of the regiments, an increasing number of slaves were bought and freed to become part of the various units. The West India Regiments served with great distinction during the Napoleonic Wars, and two of them (the 1st and 5th) participated in the Battle of New Orleans in 1815. Due to the success of the West India Regiments, during the Napoleonic Wars the British authorities decided to raise two units of Colonial Marines (naval infantrymen) made up of free blacks. A First Corps of Colonial

The British Troops in the West Indies 75

Grenadier of the 42nd Highlanders (left) and grenadier of the 92nd Highlanders (right). The dark blue and chequered bands of the bonnet are clearly visible in this picture.

Marines (150 men) existed between 1808 and 1810, while a Second Corps of Colonial Marines (three companies, gradually expanded to six) was active from 1814–16. Since most of the 'white' Royal Marines were involved in the military operations taking place in Europe, the Royal Navy badly needed some local naval infantry for service in the Caribbean. In addition to the West India Regiments and the Colonial Marines, the British raised the following black regular units in the Caribbean:

Surinam Chasseurs: Originally this was a Dutch colonial corps, created in 1772 by recruiting 300 free blacks from the territory of Surinam (located north of Brazil on the Caribbean coast). The corps' main function was to counter the local maroons, slaves who had escaped from their plantations and lived as fugitives in clandestine communities. When the British first occupied Surinam from 1799–1802, the Black Chasseurs continued to serve under the new colonial authorities. In 1804, British military forces occupied Surinam again and decided to expand the existing black unit, which assumed the new denomination of Surinam Chasseurs, with five companies (instead of the previous three). Officers and NCOs of the corps were all whites, like in the West India Regiments. The unit continued to exist even after Surinam was given back to the Dutch following the end of the Napoleonic Wars, albeit adopting a new denomination.

Martinique Brigades: Despite their denomination, these were two small corps of black rangers consisting of just five to eight men each. Raised on the island of Martinique in 1810, they were charged with opposing the local communities of maroons.

Dominica Rangers: Raised in 1814 from free blacks on the island of Dominica, this corps was charged with ending the illegal activities of the maroons. Like the previous unit, it had a very small establishment.

Black Garrison Companies: These were formed with veterans of the West India Regiments who were no longer fit for active service. The 1st Company, raised in 1813 from soldiers of the 2nd, 5th and 7th West India Regiments, was disbanded in 1817. The 2nd Company, raised in 1815 from soldiers of the 5th and 7th West India Regiments, was disbanded in 1817.

During the Napoleonic period, the British colonies in the West Indies were also garrisoned by some small white units that had very peculiar histories. The following corps were active during this period:

Royal Dutch Battalion and Royal Dutch Artillery: When the British occupied the Dutch colony of Surinam, the local white garrison was taken into British pay. It was reorganized as an infantry battalion known as the Royal Dutch Battalion and two artillery companies called the Royal Dutch Artillery. In December 1802, when Surinam was returned to the Dutch, these units were transferred back to the Dutch Army. In 1804, when the British occupied Surinam for the second time, the local white troops were absorbed into the Surinam Chasseurs.

Independent Companies of Foreign Artillery: This corps was created in 1798 by assembling together the artillery companies of two mercenary units that had been sent for service in the West Indies. Most of their soldiers were Germans, while a good number of the officers were French royalists. In 1803, the two companies were disbanded and absorbed into a newly created Royal Foreign Artillery corps which comprised a total of three companies. The latter were all disbanded in 1817.

York Light Infantry Volunteers: This unit was formed in 1803 by using Dutch prisoners of war who had been captured in the Caribbean and who wished to serve under the British flag. Initially named the Barbados Volunteer Emigrants, in 1804 it received the new denomination of the York Light Infantry Volunteers and was reinforced with the arrival of French deserters coming from Spain. This corps was one of the best foreign units in British service operating in the West Indies, since it always maintained its original establishment of ten companies and fought with distinction on several occasions. It was dressed in dark green, like the Rifles, and was finally disbanded only in 1817.

European Garrison Companies: These were raised from white soldiers operating in the West Indies who were no longer fit for active service. The 1st Company was created in 1803 and disbanded in 1817, while the 2nd Company was formed in 1803 and disbanded in 1814. The former members of these companies were absorbed into the 2nd Black Garrison Company, analyzed above.

Royal West India Rangers: This corps was formed in 1806 from members of the Royal African Corps, a British colonial unit created for service in Western Africa that will be covered in the following chapter. Initially consisting of eight companies, it reached the establishment of ten companies in 1807 after absorbing several British convicts and French prisoners of war. The unit had dark green 'rifle' uniforms and was disbanded in 1819.

78 Wellington's Infantry, 1805–1815

Two Highlanders depicted in France during 1815. The left figure, with white jacket, is presumably a musician.

Royal York Rangers: This unit, created in 1807, was also formed from members of the Royal African Corps. Mostly made up of British and foreign convicts, originally it had six companies that were later expanded to seven. Disbanded in 1819, it had both a light infantry nature and a penal character like the previous unit.

York Chasseurs: Created in 1813, it mostly consisted of Irish deserters and thus was a 'penal' unit. It took part in several combat operations in 1815, before being disbanded in 1819.

Member of the Corps of Loyal North Britons, a military association created in London during 1803 by local Scottish residents. In this case the kilt has been replaced by white trousers, but a plaid made of tartan cloth is carried over the knapsack.

The British colonies in the West Indies also had their local units of militia, which were made up of all the able-bodied white colonists living in their territory as well as the free blacks who were available for military service. Generally speaking, the white settlers served in cavalry units or as officers for the infantry corps, while the free blacks made up the rank-and-file of the foot units. Like in Canada, the militiamen were required to provide their own uniforms and personal equipment; in addition, they had to train on a regular basis, at least once in a month. In case of emergency, the militia could be augmented with the inclusion of slaves, but these could not be armed with firearms (they could receive only pikes). All the British militia organized in the Caribbean also acted as constabulary forces, since slave uprisings could take place at any moment. One of their primary tasks was to hunt maroons and runaway slaves in order to keep order in the plantations. The following militia were active in the region:

Antigua: The militia of this colony, at the beginning of the nineteenth century, comprised several units. These consisted of two infantry regiments, one independent infantry company, one squadron of dragoons and one battalion of artillery. The two major infantry units were known as the Red Regiment and Blue Regiment, from the distinctive colour of their uniform's facings.

Bahamas: Each of the islands making up the Bahamas archipelago had its own militia units. Nassau could count on one infantry regiment with 500 men, one troop of light dragoons and one artillery company made up of volunteers. Crooked Island had one infantry and one artillery company, while Exuma and Long Island had one infantry company each.

Barbados: This colony had quite a large militia, comprising one infantry regiment for each of the eleven parishes that made up the territory of Barbados. In addition to these, which consisted of about 3,330 militiamen – including 400 free blacks – there was also a small cavalry unit of sixty troopers known as Life Guards. Of the eleven infantry regiments, that organized in the parish of Bridgetown (Barbados' capital) had an elite status and bore the denomination of the Royal Regiment of Militia.

Grenada: The militia of this island, mustering 1,200 men, consisted of five infantry regiments plus one troop of light dragoons and two companies of artillery. A smaller nearby island, part of the same colony, had its own independent infantry regiment.

Jamaica: This colony had the largest militia of all the British territories in the West Indies, which consisted of around 8,000 men and included at least 3,000 free blacks. They were organized on eighteen infantry regiments, three regiments of cavalry (one for each county) and several artillery companies. Over time, some independent rifle infantry companies were also organized. Temporary companies were occasionally formed from local natives and loyal maroons, in order to clamp down on the illegal activities of runaway slaves.

Saint Kitt's: The militia of this colony consisted of just two infantry regiments, known as the Windward Regiment and Leeward Regiment.

Saint Vincent: This British possession had two regiments and five independent companies of infantry, as well as one troop of cavalry and a company of artillery.

Tobago: In 1803, the militia of this colony was reorganized to comprise one infantry regiment with nine companies, one troop of cavalry and one company of artillery.

Trinidad: This British territory had a relatively large and well-organized militia consisting of three regiments and eight independent companies of infantry, one regiment of light dragoons, a regiment of hussars, three corps of mounted chasseurs and one brigade of artillery. One of the infantry regiments, the Royal Trinidad Infantry, and the various cavalry units were all made up of white settlers, while the other corps were mostly made up of free blacks under white officers.

Chapter 8

The British Troops in Africa and Australia

At the beginning of the nineteenth century, the British had just a few colonial possessions of modest dimensions in Africa. These were located on the Gulf of Guinea in Western Africa and consisted of small footholds extending along the coast. British possessions included portions of present-day Gambia, Ghana (at the time known as Gold Coast) and Sierra Leone. It was in the latter territory that the British had their main base of Freetown. In August 1800, the British authorities decided to raise a regiment for the defence of their West African possessions, which became known as Fraser's Corps of Infantry from the name of its commander. Since no British soldier wanted to serve in such dangerous colonial outposts, the new infantry unit had to be raised as a penal corps from deserters and condemned men who had no choice but to join the regiment in order to regain their freedom. Once in Africa, the unit (of two companies) was enlarged with the inclusion of local black recruits and participated in various military operations conducted against the French colony of Senegal. In 1804, the regiment (now based on ten companies) received the new denomination of the Royal African Corps. Two years later, some of its men were detached to form a new unit to serve in the West Indies, the Royal West India Rangers. In 1807, the unit changed its name again, becoming the Royal York Rangers; in that same year, some of its men were detached too to form a new unit in the West Indies. The latter was given the title of the Royal York Rangers, while the original corps remaining in Africa went back to its previous denomination of the Royal African Corps. From 1810, the Royal African Corps was permitted to recruit significant numbers of black soldiers, thus partly changing its original penal corps character. In 1817, six companies of the Royal Africans were sent to South Africa, where they were disbanded in 1821. The four companies remaining in West Africa were disbanded in 1819.

In 1806, the British expanded their colonial possessions in Africa by capturing the Cape of Good Hope in South Africa from the Dutch. The Cape was located in a strategic position, controlling the most significant commercial and naval routes connecting the Atlantic Ocean with the Pacific. For this reason, it had to be well garrisoned. The Dutch East India Company had established a permanent military garrison at the Cape of Good Hope in the last decades of the eighteenth century. Initially, the Dutch organized a Corps of Bastard Hottentots in 1781, which was

Infanterie Légère de Lowenstein

Soldier of Lowenstein's Chasseurs, the light infantry unit of German mercenaries that was disbanded to form the new 5th Battalion of the 60th Regiment of Foot.

made up of local black recruits of mixed ancestry (half white and half Hottentot, the latter being the main indigenous component of South Africa). This early unit, with 400 soldiers, was disbanded in 1782 after the French Pondicherry Regiment arrived in South Africa to garrison the colony. Both the Netherlands and France were at the time at war with Britain as part of the American Revolutionary War and the Fourth Anglo–Dutch War. The French were worried that the British Royal Navy could easily capture the Cape from their Dutch allies, and consequently sent one of their colonial regiments (raised for service in Pondicherry in French India) to garrison the colony. In 1786, after the French troops left South Africa, the Dutch replaced them by recruiting a unit of German mercenaries, which, due to the origins of its members, was known as the Wurttemberg Cape Regiment. This unit, based on ten companies, was a very short-lived corps and served in South Africa only until 1791, when it was transferred to India. In 1793, the Dutch re-formed their Corps of Bastard Hottentots, which this time was named the Pandour Corps (numbering just 200 soldiers).

In 1795, the British occupied the Cape of Good Hope for the first time, and during the following year they reorganized the Pandour Corps as the new Hottentot Corps, with 300 men. In 1801, the corps was expanded to become a regiment with ten companies, which was designated the Cape Regiment. Following the Peace of Amiens, the Cape of Good Hope was returned to the Dutch, who maintained the Cape Regiment in service but changed its denomination twice during the following years (first renaming it the Corps of Free Hottentots and then the Hottentot Light Infantry). In 1806, the British conquered the Cape again and reorganized their Cape Regiment. This now had ten companies, whose officers and NCOs were all whites, while the rankers were recruited from the Hottentots. The latter were considered perfect light infantrymen, since they were used to living and fighting in the South African bush. The original unit was later expanded with the addition of a light cavalry troop. In 1817, the bulk of the Cape Regiment was disbanded, although the cavalry troop was retained and was reorganized in 1827 to form the famous Cape Mounted Rifles.

In 1787, the British First Fleet departed from Portsmouth to found a penal colony in Australia. This was the first permanent settlement of the new British colony, which had been discovered by Captain James Cook in 1770 and only started to become important for the Crown after the Thirteen Colonies were lost due to the American Revolution. To guard the convicts transported on the First Fleet and garrison the future penal colony, a unit known as the New South Wales Marine Corps was formed. This consisted of 160 Royal Marines (organized in four companies), who volunteered for service in Australia, which at the time was known as New South Wales. The New South Wales Marine Corps acted as the sole garrison of Australia until 1791–92, when the New South Wales Corps was formed. The latter had started to be raised in Britain in 1789, as a regular infantry corps to make up the permanent garrison of New South

Officer (left) and soldier (right) of the 95th Rifles. The officer's dress included a Tarleton helmet and a light dragoon jacket with frontal frogging; the headgear was soon replaced by a standard shako.

Wales. It initially consisted of just 300 soldiers in three companies, the small size of the establishment explained by the fact that very few British soldiers were willing to serve in such a distant and little-known colonial outpost. After arriving in Australia, the corps was expanded to four companies with the enlistment of 100 former members of the New South Wales Marines who had decided to remain in Australia.

The early colonization of New South Wales proved very difficult, since local agriculture was struggling. In addition, there was a chronic shortage of money, that soon led to the adoption of rum as the main medium of local trade. The officers of the New South Wales Corps were able to buy all the imported rum that reached the colony and exchange it for goods or labour at very favourable rates. Consequently, the unit soon became known as The Rum Corps. A new governor attempted to limit these illegal practices in 1795, but met with very little success and the general situation of the colony started to improve only around 1800. In March 1804, a major revolt of Irish convicts erupted in New South Wales and menaced Sydney, which at the time was only a very small settlement. The New South Wales Corps reacted rapidly and defeated the rebels at the Battle of Vinegar Hill. Four years later, the soldiers of the British garrison revolted against their own authorities, who were by now strong enough to punish all the crimes deriving from the illegal commerce of rum. This 'Rum Rebellion' achieved some success and led to the creation of a military government in New South Wales, which remained in place until 1810. In 1809, however, a new governor was sent to Australia together with the 73rd Regiment of Foot, and order was gradually restored in the young colony. In 1810, the New South Wales Corps, which had been transformed into the regular 102nd Regiment of Foot since 1808, was recalled to Britain, apart from 100 veterans and invalids who were retained for garrison duties in New South Wales. The regiment took part in some minor actions during the War of 1812 against the USA. The new garrison of Australia was made up of the 73rd Regiment of Foot until 1814, when it was replaced by the 46th Regiment of Foot.

Chapter 9

The British Troops in India

The British had built a significant presence in India from the middle of the eighteenth century, particularly after the Battle of Plassey in 1757. Until then, other European colonial powers such as France and Portugal had exerted a greater influence over India than Britain. Since the time of its first territorial acquisitions in the Indian subcontinent, the British government had not annexed any Indian territory as a direct possession of the Crown; from a formal and practical point of view, British territories in India were all under the control of the East India Company. Established in 1600, the East India Company was a joint-stock venture that originally had as its main objective that of trading with the rich countries of the Asian continent. Like its Dutch equivalent operating in present-day Indonesia, the British East India Company gradually emerged as a regional power in Asia and expanded its commercial influence by using political and military measures. Over time, the British traders started to occupy several important cities in India as well as various tracts of coastline. All these new territories were to act as outposts for the economic activities of the Company, and were also the centres from which the British could exert their influence over the local Indian rulers. By the middle of the seventeenth century, with the decline of the great Moghul Empire, India was fractured into a multitude of independent princedoms. These had outdated armies using traditional Indian weaponry and tactics, which were no match for the modern military technologies employed by the British. Consequently, the East India Company gradually used its great resources to transform several of the Indian native states into protectorates. Thanks to the signing of favourable treaties concerning trade, the British acquired direct control over an increasing number of cities and territories. After the great victory of Plassey, with which the French were expelled from most of India, the British expanded their possessions towards the interior of the subcontinent.

As a result, during the following decades, the East India Company was forced to reorganize its military forces: these, initially very small, had as their main task that of protecting the commercial interests of the Company and garrisoning its territorial possessions. Since their foundation, the military forces of the Company included a number of native soldiers, which were recruited with the help of local rulers who were allies of the Company and made up a private military organization that was not part

From left to right: officer of the 95th Rifles, soldier of the 95th Rifles and soldier from the 5th Battalion of the 60th Foot. The officer wears a hussar-style pelisse on his left shoulder; this item of dress, typical of light cavalry, was very popular among light infantry officers.

of the British Army. On many occasions, the European and native components of the Company's military forces cooperated well together and proved their efficiency on the field of battle. With the reorganization that followed Plassey, they also started to have significant numbers and their standards of service became comparable to those of contemporary European armies. The military units in the service of the Company could be European, made up of soldiers from Britain, or native corps recruited from the local population but having British officers. The Indian soldiers serving European powers, be they Hindus or Muslims, were commonly known as sepoys. Generally speaking, the European soldiers recruited by the Company in Britain were not of the same quality as those who served in the regular British Army, which offered better conditions of service to potential recruits and thus the best elements wishing to serve in the military usually entered the ranks of the regulars. Most of the British soldiers serving under the flags of the Company were individuals who had decided to leave their country in search of an opportunity, and who lived at the margins of society. Some of them had experienced problems with justice while others had no choice but to enlist as soldiers of fortune in order to earn a living. Members of the European military units did, however, also comprise significant numbers of whites who were recruited in India from all the European adventurers or mercenaries who were searching for employment. Swiss, German, Dutch and even French recruits were the most common to find, but there were also individuals of mixed ancestry (half European and half Indian). Discipline and training of these soldiers were not the same as their equivalents serving in the British Army, but on most occasions these men proved to be reliable fighters. A good number of them had a clear idea of what military discipline was, since it was not uncommon for a soldier from the regular army to decide to become part of the Company's military forces after his Indian period of service had ended. Life in India was cheaper than in Britain, and the risks faced while serving under the flags of the Company were less than those experienced while serving in the regular army.

At the beginning of the nineteenth century, the territorial possessions of the East India Company were organized into three autonomous presidencies: those of Madras, Bengal and Bombay. Each of these had their own army, comprising several military units. During the Napoleonic Wars, the European infantry of the East India Company consisted of three regiments, one for each of the presidencies. It is important to remember, however, that these units (despite their denomination) had the numerical consistency of only a single battalion and that their ten companies usually served as independent detached units. These three regiments were the following:

– Royal Madras Fusiliers
– Royal Bengal Fusiliers
– Royal Bombay Fusiliers

The units of 'native' infantry could trace their origins back to the early irregular bands of mercenaries that were organized by the Company in India during the first decades of colonization. After Plassey, these irregular corps were gradually transformed into regular military units and their members received the denomination of sepoys. They started to wear uniforms of European cut, and received modern firearms as well

Rifleman of the 95th Regiment of Foot. This picture shows very clearly the horn carried on the back (which contained additional black powder) and the wooden canteen painted in pale blue (with the regimental number in white).

Sri Lanka. The 3rd Ceylon Regiment was created, in 1805, followed by the 4th in 1810. The first unit organized by the British on Ceylon was the best of them, consisting of nine line companies and one rifle company, and it earned the new denomination of His Majesty's Malay Regiment. In 1814, this was transformed into an elite light infantry corps. The 2nd Ceylon Regiment had the same internal organization as the 1st, but it was mostly made up of Sinhalese soldiers; for this reason it was also known as the Ceylon Native Infantry. The 3rd Ceylon Regiment was formed with soldiers recruited from East Africa, who had already been organized since 1803 into a small Caffre Corps. The Caffre Corps was disbanded and absorbed into the new unit, which had an establishment of ten companies. The 4th Ceylon Regiment was made up of black soldiers from East Africa (many of whom had been converted by missionaries), except for a single company that consisted of Malays. It was disbanded in 1815 and absorbed into the 3rd Ceylon Regiment. In October 1804, the British also organized a corps of Ceylon Light Dragoons, mostly raised from sepoys serving in the Madras army of the East India Company. This had an establishment of 130 men, forty of whom were British. In 1801, the British also raised three companies of gun lascars for service in Ceylon, native carriers who were essential for the Royal Artillery. Most of these soldiers came from Bengal. Three companies of pioneer lascars were also formed in 1804.

The British captured the French colony of Mauritius, consisting of several islands located in the Indian Ocean, in 1810. To defend their new possession, they raised one infantry unit known as the Bourbon Regiment, consisting of two battalions; the first was to be made up of white colonists, while the second would be recruited from the local free blacks. In the end, however, both battalions were mostly recruited from purchased slaves who were bought in Madagascar. In 1812, the unit was reorganized as a single battalion with eight companies, one of which was equipped with rifles. In 1811, following the annexation of the Netherlands to the French Empire, an Anglo–Indian military force occupied the Dutch East Indies (present-day Indonesia). To patrol the large territory of Java, the most important island of the Dutch East Indies, two cavalry squadrons were raised in India in 1812. These were known as the Java Hussars and were disbanded only in 1816, when Indonesia was returned to the Netherlands. The British also raised a Corps of Amboynese from one of the local communities, consisting of one infantry battalion with 600 natives. This was also disbanded in 1816.

Chapter 10

Foreign Troops in British Service

At the outbreak of the Revolutionary Wars, the British Army comprised a single unit made up of foreign professional soldiers, the 60th Regiment of Foot, which has already been covered in one of the previous chapters. With the expansion of military operations conducted against France, however, the Crown was obliged to raise a large number of mercenary corps from foreign sources in order to augment the numbers of the regular forces and to have certain kinds of troops that were absent in the British Army, most notably light infantry. During the period 1793–1802, these were mostly made up of French Royalists who were forced to abandon their country after the execution of Louis XVI, who were collectively known as *émigrés*. Towards the end of 1794, the French Republic invaded the Netherlands and it latter into a puppet Batavian Republic, as a result of which a large number of Dutch soldiers became available for British service as foreign mercenaries. Several units were also raised from Germany and Switzerland, two areas of Europe that had always exported mercenaries and could contribute expert light infantrymen to the British cause. In 1802, with the Peace of Amiens, most of the foreign corps belonging to the 'first generation' of foreign troops in British service were disbanded. During the following years, however, several new foreign units were raised by the British Army on the new fronts where it began to operate, including Italy and the Balkans. In this chapter we will provide a brief overview of the major foreign units that served under the British flag between 1803 and 1815.

King's Dutch Brigade: In 1795, following the fall of the Dutch Republic, the *stadtholter* (chief of state) William V fled to Great Britain together with his son Frederick of Orange-Nassau. The latter was a capable military commander and soon started planning the organization of a 'Dutch Army in exile'. This force was raised from the many Dutch troops who had abandoned their home country and had entered territory of the then-neutral Prussia in order to avoid capture. Frederick's loyal soldiers moved to Hanover and were later transferred to Britain, where some of them were absorbed into foreign units serving in the British Army. During the 1799 Netherlands campaign, which ended in failure, the British captured several soldiers of the Batavian Republic. These included many deserters and mutineers who were

Foreign Troops in British Service 95

Rifleman of the 95th Regiment of Foot. The dark green colour of the uniform and the belt equipment made of black leather helped the British marksmen in concealing themselves while on the battlefield.

96 *Wellington's Infantry, 1805–1815*

united with the Dutch soldiers already in Britain to form a large and independent Dutch military corps. This was known as the King's Dutch Brigade and was organized on the following units: four regiments of line infantry with eighteen companies each, one regiment of jägers with eighteen companies, one battalion of artillery with six companies and a small engineer corps with one company of pioneers. The Dutch Brigade, comprising some 5,000 soldiers, was commanded by Frederick of Orange-Nassau. In November 1800, the engineers/pioneers were absorbed into the artillery and a second artillery battalion with four companies was created. In addition, the two light companies of each line infantry regiment were detached to create two new jäger battalions with four companies each. In 1802, due to the Peace of Amiens, the Dutch Brigade was disbanded without having seen action.

Dutch Light Infantry Battalion: This was organized in January 1814 from Dutch prisoners of war stationed in Britain. It consisted of a single battalion with 1,000 men, and soon became part of the re-formed Dutch Army as the 2nd Line Infantry Battalion.

Dillon's Regiment: Raised in 1795, this initially consisted of two battalions with five companies each and was mostly made up of Irish soldiers who had served in France's Royal Army. During the Napoleonic Wars, however, it came to comprise men of twenty-two different nationalities. In 1812, it had an establishment of 1,200 soldiers and five of its companies were sent to serve in the Iberian Peninsula. The regiment was disbanded in January 1815.

Froberg's Regiment: Recruited in the Balkans in 1806, it initially had 500 men and was sent to Malta in order to be part of the local garrison. In April 1807, the unit mutinied and was disbanded a few weeks later.

Foreign Recruits Battalion: This corps was raised in Spain in 1810, from deserters and prisoners of various nationalities. It was used to create the 8th Battalion of the 60th Regiment of Foot.

Chasseurs Britanniques: This light infantry unit was created in 1801 by absorbing the remnants of several *émigré* corps that had just been disbanded. Initially, it consisted of just six companies, but in 1803, it absorbed all the French Royalist soldiers who continued to serve under the British flag and thus could be expanded to a standard establishment of ten companies. Sent to the Iberian Peninsula after having absorbed several French prisoners of war, it served with distinction under Wellington during several important battles. The unit was disbanded in 1814. In addition to the Chasseurs

Foreign Troops in British Service 97

Soldier of the 51st Regiment of Foot. The new light regiments created by converting line infantry units retained their previous uniforms, except for a few details (including the green cords wrapped around the shako).

Britanniques, the French Royalists also formed two Foreign Invalids Companies between 1801 and 1814.

Malta Coast Artillery: This small corps consisted of two companies that were charged with manning the coastal batteries of Malta. It was formed from local militiamen in 1800 after the British reoccupied the island.

Maltese Provincial Battalions: These were raised for garrison duty on their home island in 1802 and consisted of seven infantry companies each. They were commanded by Maltese officers and were unified into a single corps in 1806, which was disbanded in 1815.

Maltese Veteran Battalion: Created in 1803, this consisted of 300 Maltese soldiers who were no longer fit for active service. Its four garrison companies were disbanded in 1815.

Maltese Military Artificers: This was another small auxiliary corps made up of Maltese soldiers. It consisted of two companies and was raised in 1806.

Maltese Police Corps: This was a small paramilitary corps, comprising around 200 men who acted as a gendarmerie for the island of Malta.

Royal Regiment of Malta: Initially raised as a two-battalion corps in 1805, it was later reduced to a single battalion with 750 men. The unit was disbanded in 1811 after suffering serious losses in various Mediterranean operations.

Royal Corsican Rangers: This light infantry corps was mostly formed by Corsican soldiers, who fought for the independence of their island from France. Raised in 1803, it consisted of ten companies and most of its officers were Corsican. The corps took part with distinction in several military operations conducted in southern Italy, before being augmented to twelve companies in 1811. After participating in the British landings at Trieste (1813) and Genoa (1814), the Royal Corsican Rangers was disbanded in 1816.

Royal Sicilian Regiment: After the French invaded the Kingdom of Naples in southern Italy in 1806, the local Bourbon royal family went to the island of Sicily, where it continued to resist against the invaders. Sicily was at that time the richest region of the Bourbons' southern Italian kingdom, and thus had copious human resources;

in addition, it could be easily defended from the French thanks to the presence of Royal Navy ships. In May 1806, the British authorities in Sicily started raising a light infantry battalion from Sicilian volunteers. This was gradually expanded to ten and later twelve companies, becoming a regiment in 1809 and serving as part of Sicily's garrison until being disbanded in 1816.

Calabrian Free Corps: From 1806, the main theatre of operations between the French and the Bourbons of Naples (supported by Britain) was the southern tip of Calabria in south-west Italy, which was adjacent to the eastern coast of Sicily. The French and their puppet Kingdom of Naples, ruled by French marshal Prince Joachim Murat, wanted to invade Sicily, but were never able to due to the British naval presence in the area. The Calabrian Free Corps was organized in 1809 from Bourbon subjects of Calabria who were still loyal to their royal family. Initially, it consisted of just four companies, but since the Calabrian mountaineers were probably the best light infantrymen in the Mediterranean region, it was rapidly expanded to fifteen companies. Six of these served with distinction under Wellington in Spain, six were sent to the Ionian Islands as garrison troops and three remained in Sicily. In 1814, after taking part in the British occupation of Genoa, the Calabrian Free Corps was disbanded.

Italian Levy: There were thousands of Italian prisoners of war in Britain in 1810, who were against Napoleon and had been enlisted in his Italian troops by force. In 1811, these were assembled and sent to Malta, where they were organized by Lord William Bentick into a new corps known as the Italian Levy. This initially consisted of a single infantry regiment with two battalions of four companies each. In May 1812, this 1st Italian Regiment was supplemented by a 2nd Italian Regiment, which included many soldiers from a disbanded infantry regiment of the Sicilian Army (the Reggimento 'Real Estero'). A 3rd Italian Regiment was organized in 1813, and the raising of a fourth one was planned but never realized. All three units of the Italian Levy had full establishments by early 1814. The 1st Italian Regiment served in Spain and fought with distinction during the British landings at Trieste (1813) and Genoa (1814), while the 2nd Italian Regiment also served in Spain, but was disarmed due to its poor conduct. In 1815, the entire Italian Levy fought in Piedmont against the French, who sought to invade the re-established Kingdom of Sardinia. After the end of hostilities, it was proposed to absorb the three regiments into the Piedmontese Army, but these plans came to nothing and the Italian Levy was finally disbanded in 1816.

Piedmontese Legion: Like the Bourbon house of Naples, the Savoy royal house of Piedmont had been obliged to abandon its kingdom after it was occupied by the

Officer (left) and soldier (right) of the 52nd Regiment of Foot. This unit was one of the first to be retrained as light infantry by its commander, Sir John Moore. Later, it became an elite component of Wellington's army in the Iberian Peninsula.

French troops of Napoleon. As a result, the royal family went to the island of Sardinia, which had been part of the Piedmontese state since the early eighteenth century. Here the Savoy king could reorganize his military forces and continue his resistance against the French, with the decisive support of the Royal Navy that protected Sardinia from French landings. In 1813, in view of the imminent liberation of Piedmont from French rule, the British decided to organize a new military unit made up of Italian prisoners of war (similar to the Italian Levy) that would serve under the Savoy flag. This corps, known as the Piedmontese Legion, consisted of two infantry battalions with six companies each. However, when the unit reached Genoa, hostilities had already ceased in Europe. It was subsequently made part of the newly reorganized Piedmontese Army, before being disbanded in 1817.

Ionian Islands Volunteer Militia: Until 1797, the Ionian Islands – an archipelago with a strategic position in the Adriatic Sea – had been part of the Venetian Republic. When Venice was occupied by the troops of Napoleon, the Ionian Islands were annexed to France. In 1799, a joint Russian–Ottoman fleet occupied the archipelago and the islands were reorganized as the autonomous Septinsular Republic, which was under a Russian–Ottoman protectorate. In 1807, following the Treaty of Tilsit, the Russians ceded the Ionian Islands to France. In 1810, however, the Royal Navy conquered the archipelago and occupied it until the end of the Napoleonic Wars. Between 1815 and 1864, the Ionian Islands were organized as the United States of the Ionian Islands, a British protectorate whose suzerainty was ceded to Greece only in 1864. In the years 1810–15, the British organized an irregular local militia in the archipelago, which comprised a total of 4,000 fighters, half of whom came from the island of Zante.

1st Regiment of Greek Light Infantry: After capturing the Ionian Islands from the French in March 1810, the British decided to raise an infantry unit made up of local soldiers (Greeks and Albanians). This initially comprised just five companies, but was later increased to ten. The unit was disbanded in 1816, after participating in the British occupation of Genoa in 1814. Several future leaders of the Greek War of Independence fought in the ranks of this corps.

2nd Regiment of Greek Light Infantry: Organized in 1813, this unit originally had just four companies. Like in the other Greek regiment, most of its officers were Greek and not British. The unit was disbanded in 1814.

Meuron Regiment: This mercenary Swiss regiment had originally been part of the Dutch Army. Raised in 1781, it briefly campaigned with the French in South Africa during 1783, and was then stationed in Ceylon from 1786. In 1795, the regiment was captured by the British and entered in their service. Its standard establishment was of ten companies. In 1813, the unit was sent to Canada and fought in the War of 1812 against the USA. The Meuron Regiment was finally disbanded in 1816, after which many of its members settled in Canada as colonists.

From left to right: officer, soldier and corporal of the 85th Regiment of Foot. All figures are wearing the distinctive shako of the light infantry (with green plume and bugle horn badge) and have shoulder wings on their jackets.

Roll Regiment: This mercenary Swiss regiment was raised in December 1794 for British service. Initially, it had two battalions, which were reduced to one in 1798. In 1809, it absorbed 400 Swiss soldiers who had been captured in Spain and had previously served in Napoleon's military forces. Thanks to these new recruits, the regiment was expanded to twelve companies (one of which was equipped with rifles). Part of the unit served with distinction in Spain, before the whole regiment was disbanded in 1816.

Watteville Regiment: This Swiss mercenary regiment was raised in 1801, and from the beginning it had an establishment of ten companies. The inclusion of several prisoners of war enabled the formation of two additional companies in 1810. During 1813, the Watteville Regiment was transferred to Canada for service in the War of 1812 against the USA. The unit took part in several of the most important battles fought during this conflict. Although it was finally disbanded in 1816, some of its members settled in Canada as colonists.

Chapter 11

The King's German Legion

Among all the foreign troops at the service of Britain during the Napoleonic Wars, the King's German Legion, or KGL, was without doubt the largest and most impressive. It was in essence a miniature army, comprising military units of every kind, and fought with great valour during many of Wellington's campaigns. The German soldiers of the KGL were considered the most professional of the British Army, together with members of other elite corps like the Foot Guards. As we have already seen, the German state of Hanover had been in a personal union with Britain since the early eighteenth century, and thus the two countries were ruled by the same monarch. In practice, however, they had different institutions and were governed as two autonomous states. Hanover, for example, had its own army and its own administration. Yet during the various European conflicts of the eighteenth century, Hanover always fought on Britain's side. Having a border with France, it was exposed to foreign invasion and had to count on British military support on several occasions in order to preserve its territorial integrity. Among the military forces of the German states, the Hanoverian Army was one of the most efficient and professional. At the outbreak of the Revolutionary Wars, it comprised the following units:

– One regiment of Guard infantry, on two battalions with six companies each (one of grenadiers, five of musketeers), plus an artillery section with four guns
– Fifteen regiments of line infantry, on two battalions with six companies each (one of grenadiers, five of musketeers), plus an artillery section with four guns
– One regiment of Guard cavalry, on four squadrons with two companies each
– Four regiments of heavy cavalry, on four squadrons with two companies each
– Four regiments of dragoons, on four squadrons with two companies each
– Two regiments of light dragoons, on four squadrons with two companies each
– One regiment of artillery, on two battalions with five companies each
– One miner and sapper company
– One pontoon and pioneer company

It is interesting to note that the Hanoverian Army, albeit being German, lacked light infantry troops in 1793, just like the British. During the war with France, however,

Soldiers of the King's Dutch Brigade, from left to right: fusilier of the 1st line infantry regiment, light infantryman of the 2nd line infantry regiment and jäger of the light infantry regiment. The uniform of the line infantry was of clear British cut, but had dark blue as its main colour.

one of the line infantry regiments was converted into a light infantry corps. This was structured on two battalions with six companies each, two of jägers (armed with rifles) and four of standard light infantrymen. In addition, several grenadier companies from the existing infantry regiments were detached from their original units and assembled together in order to form three elite battalions of grenadiers (each of these having just four companies). In 1803, after hostilities resumed between Britain and France, Hanover was invaded within a few days by Napoleon. Isolated and surrounded by hostile territories, it was practically impossible to defend. The Hanoverian Army was formally disbanded, but thousands of its members were willing to continue the fight against France under the flags of their royal family. Consequently, in August 1803, the British government issued a proclamation that invited all former members of the Hanoverian Army to join the ranks of the British military. The German volunteers were assembled into a new corps known as The King's Germans, which preserved the traditions of the recently disbanded Hanoverian Army. During the following weeks, hundreds of volunteers responded to the call and started to leave Germany. Most of them were embarked in the port of Husum on the North Sea and reached England within a few days. There were so many volunteers from Germany that it soon became clear that a new fighting force comprising all arms could be formed. The depot of the new corps was initially placed on the Isle of Wight, but it had to be transferred to Portsmouth because of the increasingly large number of recruits coming from Hanover. By December 1803, this new unit of the British Army had received its official denomination of the King's German Legion.

Throughout 1804, the KGL continued to expand with the arrival of new volunteers, and was gradually organized as a perfectly trained military force. By the middle of 1805, it had a stable structure that comprised the following units:

- Four battalions of line infantry
- Two battalions of light infantry
- One regiment of dragoons
- Two regiments of light dragoons
- Three companies (batteries) of foot artillery
- Two companies (batteries) of horse artillery
- An engineer corps (made up of a few specialized officers)

The internal organization of these units was exactly the same as their British equivalent. Officers were mostly German, and the discipline of the rankers was absolutely excellent. The two battalions of light infantry had one-third of their members armed with rifled carbines, the rest being equipped with light infantry smoothbore muskets. Each of the line infantry battalions included an elite platoon of sharpshooters (fifty men), who were armed with rifles.

In 1805, while Napoleon was fighting against the Austrians and Russians in Central Europe, Britain assembled an expeditionary force with the objective of reconquering

108 *Wellington's Infantry, 1805–1815*

Soldier of the Corsican Rangers. This regiment of Corsican light infantrymen was uniformed very similarly to the 5th Battalion from the 60th Regiment of Foot.

were disbanded during the early part of 1816. Most of the officers and men who had served under Wellington for so many years decided to enlist in the new Hanoverian Army, which was still in the process of being reorganized. The many battle honours of the glorious KGL were inherited by the new Hanoverian units, which acquired a great amount of competence and experience thanks to the inclusion of the KGL veterans. Thanks to the new recruits from the disbanded KGL, the Hanoverian Army of 1815 was structured as follows:

– Nine battalions of line infantry
– One battalion of light infantry
– Thirty battalions of militia infantry
– Three regiments of hussars
– Three companies (batteries) of foot artillery

The ten regular infantry battalions were grouped with three battalions of militia infantry each, in order to form larger infantry corps with four battalions each.

Chapter 12

Uniforms and Equipment

Of all the infantrymen of the various European armies, the British troops of 1800–15 probably wore the smartest and most distinctive uniforms of their age. These were very practical and modern for the time, especially when compared with those used by other armies that were still produced according to the military fashions of the eighteenth century. Red – the characteristic colour of the British infantry since Cromwell's New Model Army – was retained for most of the regiments, but as we will see, several of the new light infantry corps received some very innovative uniforms of a dark green colour. Several of the foreign corps in the British Army did not wear the standard red dress of the line infantry, thereby creating a quite distinctive appearance. Here we will provide a basic description for each item of dress that was used by the British foot troops during the Revolutionary and Napoleonic Wars period.

Headgear

The standard headgear for the officers was the cocked hat, which had changed its original shape of three folds (the tricorn) in order to become a bicorn with two folds. This change took place during the last decades of the eighteenth century, to the point that by 1800 all British officers wore the new bicorn. The left turn-up of the bicorn held a black cockade, which was held in place by a loop and a button of the same colour. During previous decades, the cocked hats had always featured a metallic lace around their external edges, but by 1800 this had disappeared from the standard bicorn of the British infantry. Above the black cockade there was a plume, whose colours indicated the type of company in which an officer was serving. A plume that was red at the bottom and white at the top indicated a centre company, an entirely white plume signified a grenadier company and an entirely green plume a light infantry company. The bicorn was worn with the loop over the left eye, and with the right wing thrown a little forward. Sometimes the loop could be in the distinctive colour of the regiment, but this practice became popular only during the second half of the Napoleonic Wars. Each cocked hat had two cords that passed around its crown to tighten it or pull in the sides, but over time these became purely decorative. The cords were golden, and at their ends there was a tassel of the same colour. Each cord passed through the loop

Uniforms and Equipment 111

Officer of the Greek Light Infantry, with the ornate 'romantic' dress prescribed for his rank. The neo-classical helmet and greaves were very Greek, as well as the fustanella kilt.

of the other, with the golden tassel hanging from the lock in the hat. To prevent the bicorn from falling off, two narrow tapes were sewn into its lining and passed down (around the back of the head) to be joined by a hook-and-eye. In 1811 the cocked hat was replaced as the standard headgear of the officers by the shako, which had been issued to NCOs and the rank-and-file soldiers since February 1800. Until that time, the rankers had also worn the bicorn, albeit with some minor differences from that described above (for example, in the colour of the cords).

Before the introduction of the shako, the British infantrymen had already tested an alternative headgear to replace the old bicorn. This was a black round hat made of felt, with a broad curved brim edged with tape and supported by laces coming from the crown. It had a black band wrapped around the base and a cockade of the same colour placed on the right side of the crown. Over the cockade there was a plume, which was in company colours. During the Revolutionary Wars against France, the round hat became very popular, since it was very practical and easier to wear than the bicorn. Notwithstanding this, it was never adopted by the whole infantry. Sometimes it could be adorned by a bearskin crest, running from front to back like the helmets of the light cavalry.

The British Army's M1800 shako was commonly known as the stovepipe shako because of its distinctive shape. Its introduction was innovative for its time, since the British Army was one of the first in the world to adopt the shako as its standard headgear. The French Army of Napoleon, for example, only introduced it on a large scale in 1806. The shako was made of lacquered leather and had a flat peak on the front, and the crown had a cylindrical shape which resembled that of a stovepipe. Frequently, the M1800 shako had a black neck protector on the back, made of leather or oilcloth, which could be tucked up into the hat or hooked up when not in use. On the top of the crown there were cut feathers for officers or a worsted wool tuft for other ranks, in company colours. At the base of the feathers/tuft there was a black horsehair or leather cockade, which had a small button with the regimental number at its centre. Instead of a number, the button of grenadier companies bore a flaming grenade, while that of light companies had a bugle horn. The front of the shako held a large plate made of tin, which had a specific design die-stamped on the rear. The frontal plate of officers' shakos was secured by copper-gilt shanks, while that of the rankers' shakos had small holes at the edges in order to take thin brass wires that fastened the plate to the shako. The decorations reproduced on the frontal plate included several elements. In the top part there was a crown, on the side of which the regimental number could be placed; in the central part there was the royal cypher, surrounded by several decorative elements; while in the bottom part there was a lion, again which could have the regimental number to the side. The infantry regiments bearing the title of 'royal' in

Soldiers of the Greek Light Infantry, with their characteristic uniform having a distinct Greek national style. The regimental colour was yellow for the 1st Regiment and green for the 2nd Regiment.

their official denomination – such as the Foot Guards and some other units with a very long regimental history – had the privilege of wearing a different frontal plate. This did not have the royal cypher in the central section, it being replaced by a distinctive regimental symbol, which varied for each unit.

From 1806, a new version of the shako started to be produced, which was lighter and slightly shorter but maintained more or less all the main features of the previous version. The officers' shako had black lace around the base and a frontal plate made

Soldier of the Greek Light Infantry. In addition to his standard musket, this light infantryman has a flintlock pistol that is carried in the Albanian fashion of the time.

for fusiliers and green for light companies. The Kilmarnock could be simple, like the one described above, or have some decorative black ostrich feathers. These feathers, sewn around the stiff blue cloth of the cap, were of two different kinds combined together: the shorter 'flats' and the longer 'foxtails'. The longerm feathers curved over the shorter ones and provided the required fullness. The feathers (clipped and fastened on a stem) were worn on the left of the Kilmarnock and were held in position by a black cockade, which had a metal button that bore regimental number for centre companies, a flaming grenade for grenadier units and a bugle horn for light companies. Over time, some features of the Kilmarnock were changed: the number of black ostrich feathers was notably increased (they were also more curved towards the top of the headgear) and a plume was added on the left of the bonnet. The plume was held in place by the black cockade, and was white for grenadier companies, white over red for centre companies and green for light companies. The plumes of flank companies were longer than those of battalion companies. The 42nd Regiment of Foot was the only Highland regiment to have different colours for the plumes: entirely red for fusiliers, red over white for grenadiers and red over green for light companies. On campaign, a flat version of the Kilmarnock bonnet was frequently worn; this was dark blue and bore the black cockade near the tourie, but had no tails on the back and no chequered band. Apparently, the grenadiers of the Highland regiments wore their 'parade' fur caps (described above) much more frequently than the grenadiers of the English or Lowland regiments.

From the beginning, the light infantry corps of the British Army had distinctive uniforms and thus did not wear the same headgear as the line infantry. The 5th Battalion of the 60th Regiment of Foot was the first to have such distinctive dress, and its headgear consisted of a black Tarleton helmet for officers and a black stovepipe shako for other ranks. The Tarleton – named after Banastre Tarleton, the ruthless British cavalry leader from the American War of Independence, often depicted wearing such a helmet – had a black peak on the front and a fur crest that went across its crown from front to back. It was decorated with a band of dark green cloth with silver stripes that was wrapped around its bottom part, and by a plume of the same colour that was placed on the left side (held in position by a red cockade). The light infantry shako was black, with a small dark green plume on the front that was held in place by a red cockade, while on the front of the headgear there was also a silver bugle horn badge. Decorative dark green cords and tassels were frequently worn around the shako, while the helmet could have a silver bugle horn badge applied on the right side. After being raised, the 95th Rifles adopted the same kinds of headgear, albeit with some small differences. The cockade, for example, was black for both the officers' helmet and for the stovepipe shako. The 60th Regiment of Foot also later adopted new black cockades.

Soldier of the Watteville Regiment, wearing the original uniform employed by this corps. This had many light infantry features, being green with black facings.

When the new M1812 shako was introduced for the line infantry, the 60th Foot and the 95th Rifles maintained their stovepipe shakos as a mark of distinction from all the other foot units. The original headgear for rankers was never modified in any significant way, the only notable innovation being the unit badge worn on the front: this started to be made of brass and, in addition to the usual bugle horn, also bore the unit number. Regarding the officers, the Tarleton helmet only remained in use for a very short time since it was not practical to wear on campaign. It was soon replaced by the same stovepipe shako worn by rankers. The light infantry regiments created by converting existing line units retained their standard stovepipe shakos, which continued to be worn after the introduction of the new M1812 headgear as a mark of distinction. They followed the same evolution as the shakos used by the rifle corps, and had the same frontal badge with bugle horn. Interestingly, the light regiments created by converting former Highland line units received a peculiar version of the stovepipe shako, which had several features of the Scottish Kilmarnock. It was dark blue and had a chequered band of white, red and green exactly like the bonnet, and also had the same frontal badge as the ordinary shakos, but instead of the frontal plume it had a dark green tourie on the top.

Coat/jacket

In 1793, the British infantry was dressed with long-tailed coats, which were worn open from the neck and sloped away at the waist. The main colour of this item of dress was scarlet, with collar and cuffs in the distinctive colour of each regiment. The lapels on the front of the coat were also in this distinctive colour, while the turn-backs were white, except for those regiments that had buff as their distinctive colour (which had buff turnbacks). The skirt and linings over which the coat was worn were white for most of the regiments and buff for those that had buff facings (collar, cuffs and lapels). The scarlet coats had horizontal pockets for centre and grenadier companies, while those of the light companies were oblique. Each coat could be worn with the lapels buttoned over or folded back in order to show the regiment's colour; the former practice was popular only on campaign, and mostly among the light companies of the various regiments. This model of coat, which had not changed since the days of the American Revolution, was completely modified in 1796 in order to be much more practical and modern. Now it was to be fastened to the waist, while the lapels were retained (for the moment) but were made to button over on every occasion. The collar was also modified, becoming a standing one rather than lying flat. In October 1797, the lapels were officially abolished for all non-officers, and thus the scarlet coat of the British line infantry became a single-breasted jacket. The British Army had been one and had the same colour/decorative design as the seams' lace. The musicians of the infantry regiments were also easy to recognize on the battlefield because they wore the same shoulder wings as the flank companies. In 1812, a great change occurred in the uniforms of the musicians: all jackets were ordered to be scarlet, like those of the ordinary soldiers from each regiment, and the old practice of wearing reversed colours was abandoned.

The 5th Battalion of the 60th Regiment of Foot was the first regular light infantry unit of the British Army to wear a dark green uniform. This included a very modern and smart single-breasted jacket, with red standing collar and pointed cuffs. The piping to the front and to the short turnbacks of the jacket was red. Shoulder straps were dark green with red piping, and had dark green-and-red rolls. The rifle companies of the other battalions from the same regiment wore a slightly different single-breasted jacket: this had a dark green standing collar and pointed cuffs piped in red, entirely dark green rolls on the shoulders and dark green short turnbacks piped in red. Officers wore a completely different uniform, comprising a dark green light dragoon single-breasted jacket. This had three rows of buttons on the front, each connected by black frogging. The bottom edge of the jacket was piped in black. The standing collar and pointed cuffs were red, decorated with silver embroidering. The officers' jacket also had silver shoulder wings, piped in red and decorated with silver fringes. The uniform adopted by the new 95th Rifles in 1800 remained more or less unchanged during the Napoleonic period. This comprised a dark green jacket with three rows of buttons on the front, which soon became a distinctive feature of the rifle corps' dress. The jacket had a standing collar and pointed cuffs in black, while shoulder straps were dark green, with black piping and a crest made of black wool. By 1815, this had remained practically the same except for the addition of white piping to the collar, cuffs and shoulder straps. The officers' jacket was quite different and consisted of a dolman similar to that worn by the light dragoons. This was dark green and had three rows of buttons on the front; the buttons, however, were smaller and much more numerous than those worn on the other ranks' jacket. In addition, they were connected by black decorative frogging. Collar and pointed cuffs were black, the former being decorated by a stripe of extra black lace and the latter by an embroidering commonly known as 'Hungarian knot'.

The line infantry regiments converted to become light units retained their standard scarlet uniforms, simply adding shoulder wings to them. In the light regiments, these wings were worn as a mark of distinction by all the companies and not only by the flank companies, as in the line regiments. The officers retained their original uniforms like the rankers under their command, but very frequently these underwent some modifications that were not prescribed by official regulations. First of all, many light

Uniforms and Equipment 123

Hanoverian soldiers of the King's German Legion line infantry; they are dressed with standard British uniforms, having dark blue as their facing colour.

infantry officers wore the lapels of their jackets folded back on campaign: this was made to show the frontal plastron in the distinctive colour of the regiment. In addition, light infantry officers frequently wore a hussar-style jacket (known as a pelisse) on their left shoulder. This was usually red or grey, and had the external edges covered with fur. Thanks to its many buttons and decorative frogging, it was a very popular item of dress (albeit not being prescribed by official regulations). It was not uncommon for light infantry officers to wear a green band of cloth wrapped around the bottom part of their shako, or to use light cavalry boots instead of the usual infantry ones.

What follows is, for each foot regiment of the British Army, the distinctive colour of its uniform's facings. It is important to remember that all the units bearing the title 'royal' in their official denomination had dark blue as their facing colour.

- 1st Foot Guards: dark blue
- 2nd Foot Guards: dark blue
- 3rd Foot Guards: dark blue
- 1st Regiment of Foot, 'The Royal Scots': dark blue
- 2nd Regiment of Foot, 'The Queen's Royal': dark blue
- 3rd Regiment of Foot, 'The Buffs': buff
- 4th Regiment of Foot, 'King's Own': dark blue
- 5th Regiment of Foot, 'Northumberland': yellowish green
- 6th Regiment of Foot, '1st Warwickshire': deep yellow
- 7th Regiment of Foot, 'Royal Fusiliers': dark blue
- 8th Regiment of Foot, "The King's": dark blue
- 9th Regiment of Foot, 'East Norfolk': pale yellow
- 10th Regiment of Foot, 'North Lincolnshire': pale yellow
- 11th Regiment of Foot, 'North Devonshire': blue-green
- 12th Regiment of Foot, 'East Suffolk': pale yellow
- 13th Regiment of Foot, '1st Somersetshire': yellow
- 14th Regiment of Foot, 'Bedfordshire' ('Buckinghamshire' after 1809): buff
- 15th Regiment of Foot, 'Yorkshire East Riding': yellow
- 16th Regiment of Foot, 'Buckinghamshire' ('Bedfordshire' after 1809): yellow
- 17th Regiment of Foot, 'Leicestershire': white
- 18th Regiment of Foot, 'The Royal Irish': dark blue
- 19th Regiment of Foot, '1st Yorkshire North Riding': blue-green
- 20th Regiment of Foot, 'East Devonshire': pale yellow
- 21st Regiment of Foot, 'Royal North British Fusiliers': dark blue
- 22nd Regiment of Foot, 'Cheshire': buff

- 23rd Regiment of Foot, 'Royal Welch Fusiliers': dark blue
- 24th Regiment of Foot, '2nd Warwickshire': blue-green
- 25th Regiment of Foot, 'Sussex' ('King's Own Scottish Borderers' after 1805): deep yellow
- 26th Regiment of Foot, 'Cameronian': pale yellow
- 27th Regiment of Foot, 'Enniskillen': pale buff
- 28th Regiment of Foot, 'North Gloucestershire': yellow
- 29th Regiment of Foot, 'Worcestershire': yellow
- 30th Regiment of Foot, 'Cambridgeshire': pale yellow
- 31st Regiment of Foot, 'Huntingdonshire': buff
- 32nd Regiment of Foot, 'Cornwall': white
- 33rd Regiment of Foot, '1st Yorkshire West Riding': red
- 34th Regiment of Foot, 'Cumberland': yellow
- 35th Regiment of Foot, 'Dorsetshire' ('Sussex' after 1805): orange
- 36th Regiment of Foot, 'Herefordshire': yellowish green
- 37th Regiment of Foot, 'North Hampshire': yellow
- 38th Regiment of Foot, '1st Staffordshire': yellow
- 39th Regiment of Foot, 'East Middlesex' ('Dorsetshire' after 1807): light green
- 40th Regiment of Foot, '2nd Somersetshire': deep buff
- 41st Regiment of Foot, 'Royal Invalids': red
- 42nd Regiment of Foot, 'Royal Highland': dark blue
- 43rd Regiment of Foot, 'Monmouthshire': white
- 44th Regiment of Foot, 'East Essex': yellow
- 45th Regiment of Foot, '1st Nottinghamshire': blue-green
- 46th Regiment of Foot, 'South Devonshire': pale yellow
- 47th Regiment of Foot, 'Lancashire': white
- 48th Regiment of Foot, 'Northamptonshire': buff
- 49th Regiment of Foot, 'Hertfordshire': blue-green
- 50th Regiment of Foot, 'West Kent': black
- 51st Regiment of Foot, '2nd Yorkshire West Riding': blue-green
- 52nd Regiment of Foot, 'Oxfordshire': buff
- 53rd Regiment of Foot, 'Shropshire': red
- 54th Regiment of Foot, 'West Norfolk': yellow-green
- 55th Regiment of Foot, 'Westmoreland': blue-green
- 56th Regiment of Foot, 'West Essex': purple
- 57th Regiment of Foot, 'West Middlesex': pale yellow
- 58th Regiment of Foot, 'Rutlandshire': black

- 59th Regiment of Foot, '2nd Nottinghamshire': white
- 60th Regiment of Foot, 'Royal American': dark blue
- 61st Regiment of Foot, 'South Gloucestershire': buff
- 62nd Regiment of Foot, 'Wiltshire': buff
- 63rd Regiment of Foot, 'West Suffolk': blue-green
- 64th Regiment of Foot, '2nd Staffordshire': black
- 65th Regiment of Foot, '2nd Yorkshire North Riding': white
- 66th Regiment of Foot, 'Berkshire': yellow-green
- 67th Regiment of Foot, 'South Hampshire': pale yellow
- 68th Regiment of Foot, 'Durham': blue-green
- 69th Regiment of Foot, 'South Lincolnshire': blue-green
- 70th Regiment of Foot, 'Surrey' ('Glasgow Lowland' after 1812): black
- 71st Regiment of Foot, 'Glasgow Highland': buff
- 72nd Regiment of Foot, 'Seaforth's Highlanders': deep yellow
- 73rd Regiment of Foot: blue-green
- 74th Regiment of Foot: white
- 75th Regiment of Foot: yellow
- 76th Regiment of Foot: red
- 77th Regiment of Foot, 'East Middlesex': yellow
- 78th Regiment of Foot, 'Ross-Shire Buffs': buff
- 79th Regiment of Foot, 'Cameron Highlanders': blue-green
- 80th Regiment of Foot, 'Staffordshire Volunteers': yellow
- 81st Regiment of Foot, 'Loyal Lincoln Volunteers': buff
- 82nd Regiment of Foot, 'Prince of Wales' Volunteers': pale yellow
- 83rd Regiment of Foot, 'County of Dublin': pale yellow
- 84th Regiment of Foot, 'York and Lancaster': pale yellow
- 85th Regiment of Foot, 'Bucks Volunteers': yellow
- 86th Regiment of Foot, 'Shropshire Volunteers' ('Leinster' after 1806): yellow
- 87th Regiment of Foot, 'Prince of Wales' Irish': blue-green
- 88th Regiment of Foot, 'Connaught Rangers': yellow
- 89th Regiment of Foot: black
- 90th Regiment of Foot, 'Pertshire Volunteers': deep buff
- 91st Regiment of Foot, 'Argyllshire Highlanders': pale yellow
- 92nd Regiment of Foot, 'Gordon Highlanders': yellow
- 93rd Regiment of Foot, 'Sutherland Highlanders': yellow
- 94th Regiment of Foot, 'Scotch Brigade': blue-green
- 95th Regiment of Foot, 'Rifles': black
- 96th Regiment of Foot: buff

- **97th Regiment of Foot, 'Queen's Own Germans'**: pale yellow
- **98th Regiment of Foot**: buff
- **99th Regiment of Foot, 'Prince of Wales' Tipperary Regiment'**: yellow
- **100th Regiment of Foot, 'Prince Regent's County of Dublin'**: yellow
- **101st Regiment of Foot, 'Duke of York's Irish'**: white
- **102nd Regiment of Foot**: yellow
- **103rd Regiment of Foot**: buff
- **104th Regiment of Foot**: pale buff

Rank distinctions

Officers' ranks were shown by epaulettes that were worn on the shoulders. These could be golden or silver, like the buttons of the uniform. The number (one or two) and position (right shoulder or left shoulder) of the epaulettes indicated rank. Officers from flank companies wore their epaulettes over fringed shoulder wings, which were golden or silver to match the colour of the epaulettes. They also had the distinctive badges of their companies over the epaulettes: a flaming grenade for grenadier companies and a bugle horn for light infantry units. In February 1810, this system was partly modified, with the introduction of two new badges (one reproducing a star and the other a crown) that were used to identify an officer's rank in a more precise way. These new badges were worn on the epaulettes, which continued to be golden or silver. In addition, the epaulettes of the officers from flank companies started to be produced in a new model that also included the shoulder wings (which were no longer a separate component). Officers could also be easily recognized thanks to the use of another two peculiar elements: a crescent-shaped gorget worn on a chain under the neck (which could be golden or silver like the epaulettes) and a red silk sash that was worn around the waist. The gorget bore the regiment's number for most units, except for the Foot Guards and for some of the older regiments that had the privilege of bearing the royal cypher or a regimental symbol. The red sash was worn over the left shoulder by officers of the Highland regiments. From 1802, the rank of NCOs and soldiers started to be shown by chevrons. These pointed downwards and were placed on the sleeves midway between the shoulder and the elbow. The colour and number of chevrons indicated different ranks. Colour sergeants (armed with spontoons) were easy to recognize thanks to the presence of a special badge embroidered on top of their chevrons. NCOs also wore a red sash around the waist, which was similar to that used by officers but had a central band in the distinctive colour of each regiment. Regiments having purple or red as their facing colour had this central band in white. NCOs of the Highland regiments wore their sashes over the left shoulder. The NCOs' sashes in rifle units were crimson with a central band in black.

128   *Wellington's Infantry, 1805–1815*

Hanoverian soldiers of the King's German Legion's 1st Battalion of Light Infantry. Except for the single row of buttons on the jacket and grey trousers, the uniform is identical to that worn by the 95th Rifles.

Greatcoat

During winter months, especially on campaign, all ranks wore the greatcoat over their usual uniforms. This was of dark blue cloth for officers and of dark grey cloth for other ranks. It was double-breasted, with two rows of buttons on the front, and only the version used by officers had a coloured falling collar, in the distinctive colour of each regiment. The officers of the rifle corps wore a peculiar greatcoat, which was grey and had three rows of buttons on the front instead of two. This version had dark green falling collar and cuffs. In December 1811, the colour of the officers' greatcoats was changed to dark grey for all units, with a cape added for protection

Hanoverian soldiers of the King's German Legion's 2nd Battalion of Light Infantry. Differently from the other light infantry unit of the KGL, this one had three rows of buttons on the front of the jacket.

of the shoulders (the latter had been present on the greatcoat for other ranks since 1802). From 1806, badges of rank started to be worn on the right arm of greatcoats and the NCOs started to have the collar/cuffs of their greatcoats in their regimental colour (like the officers).

Trousers and kilts

In 1793, all the British infantrymen (except the Highlanders) wore white breeches, which were used in combination with black woollen gaiters during winter and with white ones during summer. By July 1810, however, the white breeches were completely replaced by new dark grey trousers, that could be worn under or over the black woollen gaiters. During the summer months or when serving in tropical areas, white trousers and white gaiters were usually worn. The 5th Battalion of the 60th Regiment of Foot had dark blue trousers with red piping, while the 95th Rifles had dark green trousers. The light regiments created by converting line units retained their previous breeches/trousers. NCOs and rankers of all units had black shoes, while the officers wore black leather boots. The Highland regiments wore their traditional Scottish kilts, each unit having this item of dress produced with a distinctive kind of tartan cloth. On the front of their kilts, the Highlanders wore the characteristic sporran pouch and usually carried a *sgian-dubh* (pron. ski-en du) single-edged knife. Together with black shoes, the Highlanders also wore their traditional hose socks that were made with white-and-red tartan for all regiments. During the Napoleonic Wars, for practical reasons, many Highlanders started to replace their kilts on campaign with trousers obtained from tartan cloth. These, known as 'trews', became extremely popular for everyday use, and most soldiers of the 93rd Foot had replaced their kilts with them by 1815.

Peculiar uniforms

Several infantry units, mostly foreign ones, had peculiar uniforms that were quite different from the standard ones outlined above. For each of the special categories of foot troops analysed in this book, there now follows a brief description of the dress worn.

- **Royal Veteran Battalions**: same uniform as the line infantry, with dark blue facings.
- **Canadian Fencible Infantry**: same uniform as the line infantry, with yellow facings.
- **New Brunswick Fencible Infantry**: same uniform as the line infantry, with buff facings.
- **Newfoundland Fencible Infantry**: same uniform as the line infantry, with dark blue facings.
- **Nova Scotia Fencible Infantry**: same uniform as the line infantry, with yellow facings.
- **Independent Companies of Foreigners**: same uniform as the 95th Rifles.
- **Canadian Voltigeurs**: officers had the same uniform as the 95th Rifles, but with a black fur cap; soldiers had a black fur cap, grey single-breasted jacket with black facings and grey trousers.
- **Frontier Light Infantry**: like Canadian Voltigeurs.

- **Canadian Chasseurs**: like Canadian Voltigeurs, but with a black shako.
- **Independent Company of Militia Volunteers**: like Canadian Voltigeurs.
- **Corps of Canadian Voyageurs**: no uniform; Canadian civilian clothing worn.
- **Provincial Commissariat Voyageurs**: no uniform; Canadian civilian clothing worn.
- **Québec Volunteers**: same uniform as the line infantry but with a black round hat. Purple facings.
- **Glengarry Light Infantry**: same uniform as the 95th Rifles.
- **Caldwell's Rangers**: black shako, dark green single-breasted jacket and grey trousers.
- **West India Regiments**: black round hat (replaced in 1803 by the shako), red single-breasted jacket with shoulder straps and pointed cuffs in regimental colour, small half-plastron on the chest in regimental colour, red short skirts with no turnbacks, laced buttonholes (in white), red collar piped white, white piping to shoulder straps and cuffs, and white trousers (changed to blue in 1810). Distinctive colours were as follows: 1st Regiment, white; 2nd Regiment, yellow; 3rd Regiment, yellow; 4th Regiment, yellow; 5th Regiment, green; 6th Regiment, yellow; 7th Regiment, yellow; 8th Regiment, green; 9th Regiment, yellow; 10th Regiment, buff; 11th Regiment, green; and 12th Regiment, buff.
- **York Light Infantry Volunteers**: same uniform as the 95th Rifles.
- **Royal West India Rangers**: same uniform as the 60th Foot's 5th Battalion.
- **Royal York Rangers**: same uniform as the 60th Foot's 5th Battalion.
- **Royal African Corps**: same uniform as the line infantry, with dark blue facings.
- **Cape Regiment**: same uniform as the 95th Rifles.
- **New South Wales Corps**: same uniform as the line infantry, with yellow facings.
- **East India Company's European Infantry**: same uniform as the British line infantry, but with no white lace on buttonholes and with white trousers for all seasons.
- **East India Company's Native Infantry**: same uniform as the British line infantry, but with blue turban as headgear (of different shape for each unit) and white trousers for all seasons (short during summer, with dark blue embroidering on the bottom edges).
- **Ceylon Regiments**: same uniform as the line infantry, but with blue turban for the 2nd Regiment (instead of the shako) and white trousers for all seasons. Rifle companies had the same dark green jacket of the 95th Rifles.
- **Bourbon Regiment**: same uniform as the 95th Rifles.
- **King's Dutch Brigade**: the line infantry was dressed like its British equivalent, but with reversed colours (dark blue jacket with red facings) and grey trousers; the

jägers wore dark green jacket with black facings (including frontal plastron) and grey trousers.
- **Dutch Light Infantry Battalion:** black shako, dark blue single-breasted jacket with orange facings and grey trousers.
- **Dillon's Regiment:** same uniform as the line infantry, with yellow facings.
- **Chasseurs Britanniques:** same uniform as the line infantry, with sky blue facings.
- **Maltese Provincial Battalions:** same uniform as the line infantry, with sky blue facings for the 1st Battalion and green ones for the 2nd Battalion.
- **Royal Regiment of Malta:** same uniform as the line infantry, with dark blue facings.
- **Royal Corsican Rangers:** same uniform as the 60th Foot's 5th Battalion.
- **Royal Sicilian Regiment:** same uniform as the line infantry (green facings), but with Tarleton helmet having green plume.
- **Calabrian Free Corps:** the first uniform of this corps comprised black slouch hat (with the left part of the brim turned up) having a green plume and a yellow band wrapped around the bottom part, dark blue single-breasted jacket with five rows of buttons on the front, yellow collar and cuffs decorated with dark blue embroidering and dark green trousers. In 1813, a new uniform was introduced, with black shako with dark green frontal plume, dark blue single-breasted jacket with frontal plastron piped in yellow and edged by a line of buttons shaped like a 'U', yellow collar and round cuffs, and dark blue trousers.
- **Italian Levy:** black shako, dark blue single-breasted jacket with red collar and round cuffs, red piping to front of the jacket and short turnbacks, and grey trousers.
- **Piedmontese Legion:** black shako, dark blue single-breasted jacket with red collar and round cuffs, red piping to front of the jacket and short turnbacks, and dark blue trousers.
- **Ionian Islands Volunteer Militia:** no uniform; Greek civilian clothing worn.
- **Greek Light Infantry Regiments:** red skull cap with tassel in regimental colour, red oriental-style jacket with cuffs and decorative trim in regimental colour, red shirt with decorative trim in regimental colour, entirely white fustanella (kilt), white breeches and red socks. The regimental colour was yellow for the 1st Regiment and green for the 2nd Regiment. The officers had a black neo-classical helmet as headgear, and the decorative trim of their jacket/shirt was golden. They also wore red greaves (decorated with gold) over the lower legs and knee-protectors decorated with golden lion heads.
- **Meuron Regiment:** same uniform as the line infantry, with sky blue facings.
- **Roll Regiment:** same uniform as the line infantry, with sky blue facings.
- **Watteville Regiment:** same uniform as the line infantry, with black facings.
- **KGL line infantry:** same uniform as the British line infantry, with dark blue facings.
- **KGL light infantry:** same uniform as the 95th Rifles, but with a single row of buttons on the front of the jacket and grey trousers.

Belts and pouches

The standard set of personal equipment for a line infantryman comprised a white sling for the musket, white crossbelt for the cartridge pouch, white crossbelt for the bayonet scabbard, black cartridge pouch, black bayonet scabbard, white canvas haversack, wooden water bottle (usually painted pale blue) with dark brown sling and a canvas knapsack (which could be painted in different colours) that usually bore the unit number on the back. The knapsack had two white shoulder straps, connected on the chest by a horizontal belt of the same colour. Officers had a single white crossbelt for the sword. The rifle units (5th Battalion and rifle companies of the 60th Regiment, 95th Regiment) had the following elements in black rather than white leather: carbine sling, crossbelt for the cartridge pouch and straps of the knapsack. In addition, they used a black leather waistbelt which had a small pouch on the right side (used for transporting bullets) and the bayonet scabbard on the left side. Very frequently, the riflemen also carried a white horn and a brown flask on their back, suspended on a dark green cord: the horn was used to transport additional black powder, while the flask contained priming powder for the flintlock mechanism of their carbine.

Weapons

Officers were armed with the M1796 infantry sword, except for those commanding light units, who were equipped with the M1803 infantry sword. The M1796 had a straight blade, while the M1803 had a curved blade. The M1803 sword was carried by the officers of light companies from line units as well as by all officers of rifle/light regiments. The universal weapon of the British infantrymen was the Brown Bess musket, which was used in three different versions during the Napoleonic Wars. The first and more common was the India Pattern musket, introduced in 1797 and issued to the great majority of the line regiments; the second was the New Land Pattern musket, introduced in 1802 and issued only to the Foot Guards (all regiments) and 4th Regiment of Foot; the third was the New Light Infantry Land Pattern musket, introduced in 1811 to the new light infantry units (the 43rd, 51st, 52nd, 68th, 71st and 85th Regiment). All the versions of the Brown Bess were smoothbore muskets. The 95th Rifles was the only regiment to be fully equipped with the excellent Baker carbine, a rifled weapon that started to be produced in 1800. This was also carried by the 5th Battalion of the 60th Foot, as well as by the rifle companies of all the other battalions from the same regiment. Those soldiers of the 60th Regiment of Foot not armed with the Baker carbine had the New Light Infantry Land Pattern of the Brown Bess. The Baker carbine was also employed by the light infantry battalions of the KGL, as well as

Light infantrymen of the KGL, from left to right: officer of the 1st Battalion of Light Infantry, soldier of the 1st Battalion of Light Infantry, soldier of the 2nd Battalion of Light Infantry and officer of the 2nd Battalion of Light Infantry.

by the sharpshooter platoons of each line infantry unit from the KGL. In addition to their personal musket, the colour sergeants also carried a spontoon, an old-fashioned weapon that was mostly used to defend the colours during cavalry attacks (since it was a sort of pike).

Bibliography

Barnes, R.M., *A History of the Regiments and Uniforms of the British Army* (Seeley Service, 1950)
Chappell, M., *The King's German Legion 1803–1812* (Osprey Publishing, 2000)
Chappell, M., *The King's German Legion 1812–1816* (Osprey Publishing, 2000)
Chappell, M., *Wellington's Peninsula Regiments: The Irish* (Osprey Publishing, 2003)
Chappell, M., *Wellington's Peninsula Regiments: The Light Infantry* (Osprey Publishing, 2004)
Chartrand, R., *A Scarlet Coat: Uniforms, Flags and Equipment of the British Forces in the War of 1812* (Service Publications, 2011)
Chartrand, R., *British Forces in North America 1793–1815* (Osprey Publishing, 1998)
Chartrand, R., *British Forces in the West Indies 1793–1815* (Osprey Publishing, 1996)
Chartrand, R., *Emigré and Foreign Troops in British Service 1793–1803* (Osprey Publishing, 1999)
Chartrand, R., *Emigré and Foreign Troops in British Service 1803–1815* (Osprey Publishing, 2000)
Esposito, G., *Armies of the War of 1812: United States, United Kingdom and Canada 1812–1815* (Winged Hussar Publishing, 2017)
Fletcher, I., *Wellington's Foot Guards* (Osprey Publishing, 1994)
Fosten, B., *Wellington's Infantry (1)* (Osprey Publishing, 1981)
Fosten, B., *Wellington's Infantry (2)* (Osprey Publishing, 1982)
Franklin, C.E., *British Napoleonic Uniforms* (The History Press, 2008)
Fraser, D., *The Grenadier Guards* (Osprey Publishing, 1978)
Funcken, F. and Funcken, L., *British Infantry Uniforms: from Malborough to Wellington* (Littlehampton Book Services, 1977)
Grant, C., *The Coldstream Guards* (Osprey Publishing, 1971)
Haythornthwaite, P., *British Rifleman 1797–1815* (Osprey Publishing, 2002)
Haythornthwaite, P., *The Armies of Wellington* (Arms and Armour Press, 1994)
Haythornthwaite, P., *Uniforms of the Peninsular War 1807–1814* (Blandford Press, 1978)
Haythornthwaite, P., *Uniforms of Waterloo in Colour* (Blandford Press, 1974)
Haythornthwaite, P., *Wellington's Army: the Uniforms of the British Soldier 1812–1815* (Greenhill Books, 2002)
Hofschroer, P., *The Hanoverian Army of the Napoleonic Wars* (Osprey Publishing, 1989)
Katcher, P., *The American War 1812–1814* (Osprey Publishing, 1990)
Lawson, Cecil C.P., *A History of the Uniforms of the British Army* (Littlehampton Book Services, 1974)
Reid, S., *Armies of the East India Company 1750–1850* (Osprey Publishing, 2009)
Reid, S., *British Redcoat 1793–1815* (Osprey Publishing, 1997)
Reid, S., *Wellington's Highlanders* Osprey Publishing, 1992)
Windrow, M., *Military Dress of the Peninsular War 1808–1814* (Hippocrene Books, 1975)

Index

Argyllshire Highlanders Regiment, 18

Bedfordshire Regiment, 11
Berkshire Regiment, 16
Black Garrison Companies, 76
Buckinghamshire Regiment, 12
Bucks Volunteers Regiment, 17

Calabrian Free Corps, 99
Caldwell's Rangers, 68
Cambridgeshire Regiment, 13
Cameron Highlanders Regiment, 17
Cameronian Regiment, 12
Canadian Chasseurs, 64
Canadian Voltigeurs, 62
Chasseurs Britanniques, 96, 98
Cheshire Regiment, 12
Connaught Rangers Regiment, 17
Cornwall Regiment, 13
Corps of Canadian Voyageurs, 64
County of Dublin Regiment, 17
Cumberland Regiment, 13

Dillon's Regiment, 96
Dominica Rangers, 76
Dorsetshire Regiment, 13
Duke of York's Irish Regiment, 20
Durham Regiment, 16
Dutch Light Infantry Battalion, 96

East Devonshire Regiment, 12
East Essex Regiment, 14
East Middlesex Regiment (39th), 13
East Middlesex Regiment (77th), 16
East Norfolk Regiment, 11
East Suffolk Regiment, 11
Enniskillen Regiment, 12
European Garrison Companies, 77

Foreign Recruits Battalion, 96
Froberg's Regiment, 96
Frontier Light Infantry, 62

Glasgow Highland Regiment, 16
Glengarry Light Infantry, 66, 67
Gordon Highlanders Regiment, 18

Herefordshire Regiment, 13
Hertfordshire Regiment, 14
Huntingdonshire Regiment, 13

Independent Company of Militia Volunteers, 64
Italian Levy, 99

John Russell's Regiment of Foot, 1

King's Dutch Brigade, 94, 96
King's Own Regiment, 11

Lancashire Regiment, 14
Leicestershire Regiment, 12
Lord Wentworth's Regiment of Foot, 1
Loyal Essex Volunteers, 68
Loyal Kent Volunteers, 68
Loyal Lincoln Volunteers Regiment, 17
Loyal London Volunteers, 68

Maltese Provincial Battalions, 98
Maltese Veteran Battalion, 98
Marquis of Argyll's Royal Regiment, 3
Martinique Brigades, 76
Meuron Regiment, 101
Monck's Regiment of Foot, 3
Monmouthshire Regiment, 14

North Devonshire Regiment, 11
North Gloucestershire Regiment, 13

Index

North Hampshire Regiment, 13
North Lincolnshire Regiment, 11
Northamptonshire Regiment, 14
Northumberland Regiment, 11

Oxfordshire Regiment, 14

Pertshire Volunteers Regiment, 17
Piedmontese Legion, 99, 100, 101
Prince of Wales' Irish Regiment, 17
Prince of Wales' Tipperary Regiment, 20
Prince of Wales' Volunteers Regiment, 17
Prince Regent's County of Dublin Regiment, 20
Provincial Commissariat Voyageurs, 64

Québec Volunteers, 64

Roll Regiment, 102
Ross-Shire Buffs Regiment, 16
Royal American Regiment, 15
Royal Bengal Fusiliers, 89
Royal Bombay Fusiliers, 89
Royal Corsican Rangers, 98
Royal Dutch Battalion, 77
Royal Fusiliers Regiment, 11
Royal Highland Regiment, 14
Royal Invalids Regiment, 14
Royal Madras Fusiliers, 89
Royal North British Fusiliers Regiment, 12
Royal Regiment of Malta, 98
Royal Sicilian Regiment, 98, 99
Royal Welsh Fusiliers Regiment, 12
Royal West India Rangers, 77
Royal York Rangers, 78
Rutlandshire Regiment, 15

Scotch Brigade Regiment, 20
Seaforth's Highlanders Regiment, 16
Shropshire Regiment, 14
Shropshire Volunteers Regiment, 17
South Devonshire Regiment, 14
South Gloucestershire Regiment, 15
South Hampshire Regiment, 16
South Lincolnshire Regiment, 16
Staffordshire Volunteers Regiment, 17
Surinam Chasseurs, 76
Surrey Regiment, 16
Sussex Regiment, 12
Sutherland Highlanders Regiment, 18

The Buffs Regiment, 10
The King's Regiment, 11
The Queen's Royal Regiment, 10
The Royal Irish Regiment, 12
The Royal Scots Regiment, 10

Watteville Regiment, 102
West Essex Regiment, 15
West Kent Regiment, 14
West Middlesex Regiment, 15
West Norfolk Regiment, 15
West Suffolk Regiment, 15
Westmoreland Regiment, 15
Wiltshire Regiment, 15
Worcestershire Regiment, 13

York and Lancaster Regiment, 17
York Chasseurs, 78
York Light Infantry Volunteers, 77
Yorkshire East Riding Regiment, 11